D0563857

ANCIENT PRAYER

ANCIENT PRAYER

Channeling
Your Faith
365 Days of
the Year

RACHEL C. WEINGARTEN

FALL RIVER PRESS

New York

FALL RIVER PRESS

New York

An Imprint of Sterling Publishing
387 Park Avenue South
New York, NY 10016

© 2014 by Rachel C. Weingarten

Cover image © Nikki Smith/Arcangel Images

ISBN 978-1-4351-5216-8

For information about custom editions, special sales, and premium
and corporate purchases, please contact Sterling Special Sales
at 800-805-5489 or specialsales@sterlingpublishing.com.

Manufactured in China

2 4 6 8 10 9 7 5 3 1

www.sterlingpublishing.com

Dedication

For my father's sister Rachel Weingarten, whose voice was permanently silenced at Auschwitz when she was a young girl. For the hundreds of family members who were murdered during the Holocaust; there are far too many to name each and every one. For the millions whose voices weren't heard. You are in our prayers. You are remembered. *Zachor*.

And for my mother's mother, Rivka, who died when my mother was only 12 years old. We never got to meet, but your presence is felt in the stories of faith shared by my mother. You would have been so proud of her.

Introduction

WE LIVE IN HECTIC TIMES. Between work and school, family and soccer practice, doctor's appointments and vet appointments, cooking and cleaning, elderly parents and young children, constant texts and email, we can feel overwhelmed to the point of exhaustion.

Even those raised with deep faith and daily prayer can sometimes go for days without giving proper thanks, or reflecting on the good and bad in life. Others offer up a quickly whispered prayer before a job interview or medical procedure. Some people find time to reconnect with a higher power only when things get really bad, or when they're faced with major illness or financial despair.

Popular culture is big on the idea of "gratitude." Talk show hosts advise us to count our blessings and give thanks for the good things in life. But popular wisdom leaves a lot out of the equation: the vagaries of fate that sometimes make even the simplest things seem hard. The despair that sometimes sinks in when things seem too dark to face alone. The panic over making rent or mortgage payments when work is scarce. The sadness or nagging jealousy when it seems like everyone else has a spouse or baby or car or job or new home, but you still can't seem to find your own. Even the good things—births and weddings and love and success—can make it hard to concentrate on the debt of thanks we may owe.

Why Pray?

As small children, we believe in the power, if not absolute magic, of our thoughts. We're all acquainted with the movie-magical incantation "Abracadabra." The origins of that magical phrase are debated, but my favorite theory is that it's a portmanteau of the very similar Hebrew or Aramaic words *Avra KiDavra*: "I create what I speak."

Your words are so powerful that they can break hearts or fill them with joy. Your words have the ability to comfort a wounded soul or shatter someone's confidence. Your words can act as your messengers of hope or a salve for a broken human being. But sometimes you lose your words, which is why it's helpful to know that prayer doesn't always have to be formal words. For some, prayer is meditation on a single word; "om" is among the more popular and is said to encompass every element of the universe. For others, prayer is a commitment to doing good for the world. For still others, it's losing oneself in dance or song or the rushing sound of a waterfall. The most traditional prayers, though, have words that express the full gamut of human emotion—from despair and resignation to grief or relief and joy. It's all there if you look deeply enough.

And sometimes prayer doesn't have to be anything deeper than rereading a favorite Psalm or proverb in the way that a small child needs to hear the same bedtime story night after night after night.

You create what you speak. So, speak a better world. Speak a happier and more loving life. Speak your despair and let it lead you back to your truth. And when you can't find your own words, sometimes the best thing to do is to rely on the ancient ones that have proven comforting and inspiring for millennia.

❊ ❊ ❊

Kol Hatchalot Kashot: "All beginnings are difficult." This ancient phrase is said to have originated back in rabbinic commentary on Exodus. Yet, variations of it can also be found in many different faiths and cultures. Its simplicity and depth are both astounding.

All beginnings are difficult.

Not just the beginning of a major life event or chapter. Not just a new beginning as a newlywed, first-time mother, or widow. Not just the onset of an

illness or the beginning of grad school, but also every single fresh start: starting your garden or painting a room. Cleaning your closets or getting back in touch with a long-lost friend. Accepting your child's limitations or tackling a job search. Every single beginning is difficult.

Starting a new calendar year while seeking inspiration and tightly holding onto your optimism despite the odds isn't easy—but you do it anyway. And holding onto your faith despite the odds and when you're immersed in popular culture is difficult. But you do it anyway. And searching ancient texts for secrets to modern living can be daunting—but it's also doable.

Because while we have modern conveniences never even imagined by previous generations, we also have challenges that go along with those tools. Lucky for us, we also have easier-than-ever access to the wisdom of the ages to guide us and comfort us and help us.

In modern times when people are in pain, they might tweet or blog about heartache and disappointment and grief. Or they call a therapist or spill all to a trusted friend. Or maybe they seek solace in a book that shares stories of triumph and ancient inspirational words. But where did those words originate? In the case of the Psalms, composed by

King David, they were born of a lifetime of running from enemies—from King Saul to David's own sons. Instead of becoming mired in hate at being betrayed by those he loved most, David chose to write inspirational words, ostensibly to help himself through it all. And thousands of years later, his words still guide us through tough times.

Though technology or fashion changes constantly, truth does not. The wisdom of the ages holds up for a reason. In ten years, most people will have forgotten the most popular reality TV stars or most prolific bloggers, but they will remember and quote and share the true wisdom of the ages.

How to Use this Book

*A*ncient Prayer offers daily inspiration and reminders from other generations of ways to put things into perspective using quotes from ancient biblical texts and a few ancient prayers from philosophers and poets. These are like bite-sized lessons from women and men who lived thousands of years ago, on appreciating the truly important things in life and not losing sight of the higher power that guides it all.

A new calendar year is filled with so much promise. Resolutions are made, but despite the best intentions, too many are broken. *Ancient Prayer* can be used as a daily devotional or inspirational coach in book form and followed on a day-by-day basis. It can also offer random and inspired wisdom from the ages on any page and for every stage. My hope is that you can find inspiration and comfort where and when you need it.

The Traveler's Prayer

I FEEL AS THOUGH we're embarking on a journey together—a journey of faith and reflection. And what better way to begin than with the Traveler's Prayer? In days of yore, travel used to be incredibly arduous and dangerous. For that reason, the sages composed a prayer addressing everything from wild beasts to highwaymen.

May it be your will, oh Lord, our God and the God of our ancestors, that you lead us toward peace, guide our footsteps toward peace, and make us reach our desired destination for life, gladness, and peace.

May you rescue us from the hand of every foe, ambush along the way, and from all manner of punishments that assemble to come to earth. May you send blessing in our handiwork, and grant us grace, kindness, and mercy in your eyes and in the eyes of all who see us.

May you hear the sound of our humble request because you are God who hears prayer requests. Blessed are you, our Lord, who hears prayer.

Prayer Before Prayer

L IKE THE INTRODUCTION to a really meaty book or the voiceover before a historical movie, there's a prayer some say before daily prayer service. It sets the mood or intent for the words about to be spoken. *Patach Eliyahu* is a Kabbalistic prayer that was written in Aramaic. It translates as:

Elijah opened [began speaking]

This sets the tone of the forthcoming prayer. I won't pretend to understand the subtleties involved, since I am neither a scholar of Kabbalah—the ancient mystical interpretation of the Bible—nor a Hollywood celebrity who believes myself chosen to understand this esoteric pursuit. I will, however, comment on the intricate ways that some of the words are interwoven in a style that is common to Kabbalistic tracts; words and beliefs, in turn, correspond to parts of the body. This introduction is decidedly complex, but provides a great lesson: before petitioning someone for something, or even speaking publicly, let your listener know who you are, what you're about, and what you're about to discuss.

Song of Songs 6:3

*A*NI *LIDODI, VIDODI LI* translates to:
I am my beloved's and my beloved is mine.

This particular prayer snippet is so popular that it is often engraved on wedding rings or inscribed on the top of the *Ketubah*, the Jewish marriage contract. There's so much sweet promise in that very simple statement. It's so cozy and inclusive. The world can be a great big scary place, and finding a soul mate is no simple task. But if you're lucky enough to do just that, sometimes that's all that you need: one person to belong to—who also belongs to you.

Relationships ebb and flow, but sometimes seeing the big picture or long-term goals can help. It's easy to be giddy and accepting of all when a relationship is relatively new, but as time goes by, it can become more of a chore to keep to your original commitment. Sometimes you need a simple reminder that being part of a team means arguing, agreeing, and working toward what's best for both of you.

And if you're in a more allegorical mind-set and reflect on this as having been written by Solomon to his God, it makes faith more of a partnership as well. I am yours—but you are mine too.

It's Like...

A S HUMAN BEINGS, we tend to describe our vast universe and complicated emotions by comparing them to things we already know and comprehend. And many of us suffer by comparison. Psalm 103 is full of fantastic metaphors, comparing God's mercies to all manner of wonders, such as the vastness of the earth and of a father's care for his child. Some examples are:

> *For as the heaven is high above the earth, so great is his mercy toward them that fear him.*

> *As far as the east is from the west, so far hath he removed our transgressions from us.*

> *Like as a father hath compassion upon his children, so hath the Lord compassion upon them that fear him.*

The next time that you want to tell someone just how important they are to you, consider expanding your list of descriptors to include the truly vast and wondrous.

Happiness vs. Sustenance

I SOMETIMES WONDER WHERE the commonly accepted notion of people of faith being dour originated. After all, if you even just skim the ancient texts, right next to the more serious messages are words of joy and light. In Psalm 104:15, the psalmist says:

And wine cheers the heart of man.

There is a very important place for happiness in an observant life and yes—*gasp*—sometimes that involves a glass of wine with dinner or friends. There's much talk in popular culture about finding happiness—as though if you aren't grinning ear to ear 24 hours a day you're somehow missing out on life. But Verse 15 says:

And bread sustains man's heart.

Substitute fun for wine and structure for bread and you might have a better balance. Both have their place, time, and importance in a well-balanced life.

Blessing upon Seeing an Unusual Person or Animal

W E ALL KNOW THAT there are no such things as unicorns, but what if you see an okapi, bongo, or kinkajou? Fear not: there's a blessing for that.

> *Blessed are you, oh Lord our God,*
> *king of the universe, who makes*
> *the creatures different.*

This can also be recited when seeing very unusual looking people—say a seven-foot woman or someone with features that resemble nothing we've ever seen before. Sometimes we take our homogeneous lives and standard looks for granted. This blessing can be a nice reminder of all that's different and amazing in the world.

Blessing upon Seeing an Exceptionally Beautiful Person

I HOPE YOU WON'T THINK LESS of me for this one, but my friends and I sometimes see men who are so amazingly good-looking that we joke that there should be a blessing made on them. Well, guess what? There's actually a blessing that you can say upon encountering someone who is just so incredibly beautiful as to be out of the norm.

Blessed are you, oh Lord, our God, king of the universe, who has this in his universe.

It makes me happy to think that if you happen to see an exceptionally beautiful person walking down the street, you can refer to this handy dandy prayer.

Prayer for the Sick

Part I

M I SHEBEIRACH: This phrase is from the first two Hebrew words of a short prayer made on behalf of a seriously ill person, and it means:

The One who blessed

The prayer is generally made by a close family member and usually accompanies the reading of the Torah in a synagogue. Since it's a prayer that offers great comfort, it can also be recited at the bedside of someone who is gravely ill.

The origins of the prayer are unclear, though its meaning feels very modern in scope, as it addresses not only the physical infirmities, but emotional healing as well. Quite generously, it ends with wishing speedy healing to anyone within the greater community and asks for an "Amen," so that those hearing the prayer offer their assent and shared prayer.

* * *

Part II

May the One who blessed our fathers
Abraham, Isaac, and Jacob

*And our mothers Sarah, Rebecca,
Rachel, and Leah*

Bless and heal this person
[insert the person's first name]

the son/daughter of
[it's traditional to use the mother's name
when praying for someone].

*May the Holy One, blessed be, be merciful
and strengthen and heal him/her.*

*Grant him/her a complete and speedy
recovery—healing of body and healing of soul.*

*Along with the ill, among the people of Israel
and all humankind,*

soon,

hastily,

without delay,

and let us all say: Amen.

In ancient Hebrew Testament liturgy, when something is repeated, it is usually to inspire a question or, in this case, to emphasize the importance of the issue. Not only do we want the person healed, we ask that it happens as soon as possible and without any delays. It's a charming way of trying to help rush along the healing process.

Facing Our Enemies

THOUGH WRITTEN THOUSANDS of years ago, ancient prayers are still so relevant and relatable to modern life. The settings and clothing may have changed, but the feelings, fears, and genuine concerns remain nearly identical and equally urgent.

Throughout this book, I'll share some of King David's beautifully composed Psalms. But King David's life wasn't a charmed one. He faced enemies from all sides: political, familial, and professional enemies didn't simply want to steal David's job, but also end his life.

Psalm 143 begins with David asking God for help in dealing with his enemies. He seems beaten down by life and according to him, his adversaries:

Have pursued my soul and
crushed my life to the ground

Haven't we all felt like that some days—as though hope was gone and the bad guys were winning? David's enemies clamored to take over his kingdom. For us, some days feel just as hard when we have to deal with backstabbing coworkers or bosses trying to steal credit for our work.

But David didn't simply ask God to heal his broken and crushed spirit—he wanted to add a little satisfaction to the mix:

> *Cut off my enemies and destroy*
> *all the oppressors of my soul.*

It isn't always easy keeping the faith. External influences can sometimes make ordinary bad days feel crushing. And while it's important to stress the positive and pray for better days ahead, there isn't anything wrong with sometimes hoping that the bad guys lose their power to negatively affect your life.

Free Will

EVERY SINGLE DAY of our lives, we make decisions. Some are simple—fully caffeinated or decaf, paper or plastic. Some choices say more about our personal taste, or concern the charitable causes we support. Some decisions are a bit more complicated: Do we return the extra $1.00 given to us accidentally by a grocery clerk? What if it's $5.00 or $10.00? When do the decisions go from no-brainers to something more complex?

In the movies, it's usually clear who the heroes are. In old Westerns, good guys wear white hats or a sheriff's badge. In more modern times, good guys can be men who stay true to their wives; or teenagers who resist the lure of illegal substances or friends who are bad influences.

In biblical times, things were a lot more black-and-white. In Deuteronomy 143:15, things were spelled out clearly. God says:

> Today I have set before you [a free choice]
> between life and good and death and evil.

Imagine if everything in life was that simple: Do the right thing and you'll have it made. Do the wrong thing and face death and evil.

When faced with a tough decision, sometimes it's important to try to break things down to their most basic elements. Is this a good decision? If so, for whom—for you and your family, or for the greater community, if not the world? If your gut isn't entirely comfortable with your decision, will others be negatively affected? Will you be proud to choose one thing and embarrassed of the other?

We were all given free will, and that also involves the ability to make poor decisions. If you choose to do good when you're making choices about small or basic things, it will be easier to choose wisely on the larger issues as well.

Hanna's Prayer

COUNTLESS WOMEN over the centuries face the heartache of infertility, and despite myriad medical innovations in recent years, it still isn't easy to create a new life. Facing friends with their bouncing bundles of joy can sometimes be too much to bear.

In 1 Samuel 1:10, Hanna, who is barren and brokenhearted, prays fervently for a child:

> *And she was in bitterness of soul and prayed to the Lord and wept in anguish.*

Hanna's prayers are witnessed by the high priest Eli, who sees her lips moving silently and thinks her drunk. His words are harsh as he orders her to move along. Hanna's impassioned response to Eli conveys the truth. "Oh no, sir! I haven't been drinking wine or anything stronger. But I am very discouraged, and I was pouring out my heart to the Lord."

There are a few beautiful lessons of faith to be learned from *this* part of Hanna's story. I say this part, because it's not yet the joyful ending where she became mother to the prophet Samuel. In this part Hanna considers herself drunk on sorrow and realizes that sometimes the only way to deal with a great pain is to pour your sorrow into prayer.

Release the Anger

FORGIVENESS IS A MULTIFACETED CONCEPT that differs radically from culture to culture, religion to religion, and generation to generation. In Psalm 85:3–4, the psalmist says about God:

Thou hast forgiven the iniquity
of thy people, Thou hast pardoned
all their sin. Selah. Thou hast
withdrawn all thy wrath; Thou hast
turned from the fierceness of thine anger.

I believe we're meant to learn a great life lesson from these sentences. So many people rush toward forgiveness, because they hate strife or want to be perceived as the good one in the equation, or simply want to move on as quickly as possible. But in their rush, they sometimes don't work through the issues that got them to that shared bad place. Only when wrath has truly been withdrawn, only when the fierceness of anger has truly dissipated, comes the potential to move forward without resentment.

The Song of Songs: Love

THE SONG OF SONGS, or *Shir HaShirim* in Hebrew, is one of the more well-known celebrations of love. Some say that it is simply an analogy, comparing the deep and abiding love and faith of a person and their God to that of a man and his beloved. Whatever your interpretation, the Song of Songs contains classically beautiful declarations of love that rival Shakespeare's sonnets.

> *Let him kiss me with the kisses of his mouth—for thy love is better than wine.*

What's pretty amazing about this excerpt is just how classic the sentiments are. There are so many people who declare themselves oenophiles and experts on all things grape-related. Imagine those cork dorks summing up their greatest affections by saying that their beloved has a kiss sweeter than wine. It doesn't get more emotional or romantic.

Blessing upon Meeting an Incredibly Knowledgeable Person

SOME YEARS BACK I attended an event that included an appearance by Bill Gates. I can't remember exactly what he was promoting, but it was incredible to try to understand how he expanded his knowledge to modernize technology. The punch line of this story is that Gates fumbled when discussing a particular function on one of Microsoft's more common programs. I jumped in with a quick fix and offered to teach him how to do it (true story—you can ask my sister).

At the time, I had no idea that there's an actual blessing that can be said when encountering someone who's an incredible scholar:

> Blessed are you, oh Lord our God,
> king of the universe, who has given
> of His knowledge to flesh and blood.

If you value intellect the way that I do, you may also feel that it can be a gift and blessing from above.

Keep At It

HISHTADLUT IS A HEBREW WORD for striving or trying, making an effort. More than that, this one word is used to express a powerful concept. There's the old expression that God helps those that help themselves. The word *Hishtadlut* embodies all of that and more. It's a wonderful thing to be a person of strong faith. And it's a noble thing to think that there's a power above you that is owed a debt of gratitude for your pretty amazing life. When things get bad, it's comforting to be able to pour out your heart and pray. But you must have *Hishtadlut*. You can't just think that you'll simply utter a few ancient words and expressions and have everything your heart desires. You can't just sit around praying for better. You have to work as hard as you can to *make* things better.

Spring and Hope

WHILE THE SONG OF SONGS seems ripe with romantic imagery, it also relates to hope in life and matters of faith. Using the language of lovers and springtime, the prayer almost bursts with hopeful prose. Song of Songs 1:10–13 says:

My beloved spoke and said unto me: Rise
up my love, my fair one and come away.
For the winter is past, the rain is over and
gone. The flowers appear on earth.

A few lines later, the images of love and regrowth continue:

The fig tree brings forth her green figs
and the vine in blossom give forth
their fragrance. Arise my love,
my beautiful one and come away.

It's hard not to smile—or swoon—reading such hopeful words. During bleak times or cold winter months it can be hard to hold onto hope and faith. But there's something comforting about seasons changing and the world springing back to life after even the darkest winter.

Shema Yisrael

Part I

THE *SHEMA* IS ONE OF the most widely known of all ancient texts. It's often the last prayer of the day said right before going to sleep. It's also a prayer said in dire circumstances or when one is in great danger. It's a reminder that you are not alone—even in the darkest hours—and that you can always shut out the bad things and reconnect to the highest power.

The *Shema* comprises several parts of texts found in Deuteronomy and Numbers. The first is:

> *Hear, Oh Israel, the Lord is our God,*
> *the Lord is One.*

This part is said with the right hand covering one's eyes, symbolic of being alone with one's God and shutting out distractions and external elements.

Sometimes you have to take a moment and give yourself a physical reminder to shut out the world. Covering one's eyes for the *Shema* prayer is almost like covering your eyes with a sleep mask or turning off your cell phone and taking time to look inside of yourself before turning the world back on again.

* * *

Part II

THE SECOND PART of the *Shema* prayer is whispered:

*Blessed be the Name of His glorious
kingdom for ever and ever,*

As children, we were taught that this particular prayer was a private one said by the angels directly to God, and that we say it quietly so as not to anger them or infer that we are on their level. The only day that this prayer is said out loud is on Yom Kippur, the Day of Atonement, when Jewish people fast and pray, and are considered on the same level as angels.

Much in the way that Native American tradition includes placing "dream catchers" over a bed to filter out bad dreams, a bedtime prayer offers the hope of having peaceful slumbers.

I Give Thanks

ONE OF THE FIRST PRAYERS learned by the smallest of children is *Modeh Ani*, the first prayer of the day, said when you open your eyes and are still in bed.

> *I am thankful before you, living and eternal*
> *King, for you have mercifully returned my*
> *soul within me, your faithfulness is great.*

It's interesting to note that a variation of this prayer is also recited by recovering addicts. The notion shared in both the prayer and the recovery process is the belief that all elements of the soul and psyche are returned to one's maker every single night. The hope is that only the parts that serve one best are returned each morning, leaving one with a clean slate and the chance to make things right and start over from scratch every single morning.

Giving Thanks After
Surviving Danger

*B*IRKAT HAGOMEL OFFERS THANKS for having escaped some of life's more dangerous moments, like surviving a difficult childbirth, recovering from a major illness, or returning safely to loved ones after a tour of duty overseas. It isn't one of the more common blessings. Said to have its origins in Psalm 107, the blessing itself is somewhat self-deprecating:

> *Blessed art thou, Lord our God,*
> *king of the universe who bestows*
> *good to culpable, even as He has*
> *bestowed to me all good things.*

The meaning behind this blessing is important—especially as it's meant to be a public blessing with a call and response. The one giving the blessing in essence gives thanks despite admitting to being undeserving. The congregation or witnesses then respond in kind, with the hopes that he will continue to be shown kindness. In other words, this is a public and formal way of saying, "Whew. That was close."

Nightmares and Insomnia

WHAT IS IT ABOUT NIGHTTIME that brings up all of our greatest fears and worrisome thoughts? Lest you think you're alone in these darkest hours, it's been said that even wise King Solomon had a great fear of his enemies—most especially at night. Song of Songs 3:7–8 says:

> Here is the bed of Solomon, 60 strong
> men surround it, the strongest of Israel.
> They each grasp a sword and are learned
> in the ways of war. Each man with a
> sword upon his thigh—because of
> the fear of night(s).

Some of us spritz our pillows with lavender essential oils at night in the hope of encouraging peaceful sleep. Others have a soothing glass of warm milk or cozy up to a favorite plush toy. Each of us chooses different ways to help ease out of the day and into sleep, which can sometimes be elusive or filled with worries or nightmares. There's no shame in taking comfort from nighttime rituals. Even one of the greatest figures in ancient history was so fearful of nighttime terrors that he surrounded himself with his fiercest warriors.

Multifaceted Prayers and Karma

YIGDAL IS ONE OF THOSE COOL multi-use, multi-inspirational prayers with an interesting background. It's said to have been composed by Rabbi Daniel Bar Judah (a 14th century Roman Jewish scholar) and inspired by the 13 Principles of Faith described by Rabbi Moshe ben Maimon, better known as Maimonides, a Medieval Jewish scholar and physician in 12th-century Spain.

There are 13 lines to the hymn—one for each creed. And interestingly enough, in the Jewish faith, 13 is considered a lucky number. Depending on one's origins, *Yigdal* can be a prayer recited each morning or at the end of the Sabbath service. It is sung in various tunes, depending on the time of day it is sung. It's said to have inspired both opera and Christian hymns. And best of all, in the eleventh line, *Yigdal* elucidates the notion of the karmic wheel:

> *He rewards man with kindness according to his deed—He places evil on the wicked according to his wickedness.*

In other words, this very elastic and evolving prayer reminds us that what comes around goes around.

Faith Is Where You Find It

FROM THE EARLIEST AGE I was taught right from wrong. I learned to be kind to the environment, and to try to leave this world a better place than I found it. But some days are full of calamity, global sadness, and world events that are too hard to ignore, and it can be almost impossible simply to believe. When I see continued injustice in the world and blatant hatred—even among those ostensibly sharing a faith or religion—I despair of any kind of unity. During those times, I look to nature to inspire me and sustain me. Psalm 93:4 says:

> *Above the voices of many waters,*
> *the mighty breakers of the sea,*
> *the Lord on high is mighty.*

When I'm at the ocean, listening to those mighty waves and staring at the endless expanse of water, my soul always reminds me to believe in something again.

Adon Olam

ADON OLAM, ANOTHER PRAYER called by its first two words, meaning Lord of the Universe, is another daily prayer. It is translated in several basic ways, depending on the translator, and is a wonderful poem of sorts that expresses absolute faith in the existence of a divine presence. While the prayer isn't necessarily ancient, it's attributed to numerous sources and is said to have been part of religious liturgy since ancient Babylon.

Adon Olam includes snippets of some of the most famous ancient prayers. Despite being known as one of the more lighthearted daily morning prayers, it contains incredibly powerful imagery and invokes the notion of a living God—not merely an ages-old God of legend, but one who still sustains those most in need.

> *To Him I flee in times of grief,*
> *and He is my miracle and my refuge.*

The prayer is gentle in its definition of God, not only is he merciful, but a shoulder to cry on in very dark times or as needed.

Some Golden Rules

A FRIEND OF MINE IS FOND of saying that laws exist because not everyone knows how to do the right thing; they have to be reminded. In Psalm 15, King David lists some excellent personal qualities that have stood the test of time:

> *He [that] walks uprightly, and*
> *works righteousness, and speaks truth*
> *in his heart. That has no slander upon*
> *his tongue, nor does evil to his peer, nor*
> *takes up a reproach against his neighbor.*

Though the actual wording can feel a bit old-fashioned (okay, ancient, and for the most part I updated the 'doeths' and 'speaketh' for clarity), the notion of doing the right thing for the sake of doing the right thing feels timeless. It also takes a lot of insecurity out of day-to-day life. If you know that you can rest assured in your decisions, you can feel less crowded with doubt or insecurity.

Spring Blessing on a Blossoming Fruit Tree

T.S. ELIOT WROTE that April is the cruelest month, but as someone living in a city that's mostly made up of concrete and skyscrapers, I beg to differ. April seems like the most hopeful month—everywhere you look, trees seem to be showing off their buds.

Passover, also known as the Holiday of Springtime, is one of the more well-known holidays on the Jewish calendar and usually falls in April or *Nissan*. A lesser known fact is that when nature is starting to explode into full bloom again, it's customary to make a blessing on the first flowering fruit tree that you see (better yet, to wait until you see more than one flowering tree without actual fruit), and this blessing is only said the one time each year:

> *Blessed are you, God, our Lord,*
> *King of the universe, who left nothing*
> *lacking in his world and who created*
> *in it good creations and good trees for*
> *human beings to take pleasure from.*

Everything in Its Turn

ONE OF THE MORE WELL-KNOWN passages is probably better known in its abbreviated folk song incarnation "Turn, Turn, Turn." While most of the prayers in this book are limited to snippets or quotes, this one from Ecclesiastes is so full of wisdom and insight that I've included the first eight lines in their entirety:

To every thing there is a season, and a time to every purpose under the heaven;

A time to be born, and a time to die; a time to plant and a time to pick that which is planted;

A time to kill, and a time to heal; a time to break down, and a time to build up;

A time to weep, and a time to laugh; a time to mourn, and a time to dance;

A time to cast away stones, and a time to gather stones together; a time to embrace, and a time to refrain from embracing;

A time to seek, and a time to lose; a time to keep, and a time to cast away;

A time to rend, and a time to sew; a time to keep silence, and a time to speak;

A time to love, and a time to hate; a time for war, and a time for peace.

* * *

WE LIVE IN SUCH FAST-PACED TIMES that it can be tempting to rush through not only the bad moments, but also the good ones. How many people do you see snapping photos of events but forgetting to allow themselves to be in the moment? How many times do you think about what you want to post about something, rather than living it?

Life is for living. And trying to rush through any of it means that you're depriving yourself of the experience, opportunities for growth, or future healing. Don't rush. There's a right time for whatever it is that you're going through.

Girl Power!

Part I

LONG BEFORE POP MUSIC girl groups extolled the virtues of female empowerment through song, biblical heroes such as the Prophetess Deborah were using their words and voices to change ancient history. There are so many incredible takeaways from Deborah's story and prayers, which offer her own history as well. The Song of Deborah (Judges 4–5) says:

> And she sat under the palm-tree of Deborah
> between Ramah and Bethel in the hill
> country of Ephraim; and the children
> of Israel came up to her for judgment.

In a time when law was decided and decreed by judges, Deborah was one of the most respected judges. She worked from home under her date tree. In our own times, it can still be hard for women to carve out careers for themselves under their own terms. Deborah did both.

Deborah's story is shared with that of Barak, the general who raised and commanded Deborah's army against the Canaanite King Jabin and his fierce army. While Barak's army contained 10,000 men, they credit their defeat of their enemies with the pairing of prayer and military prowess. When Deborah initially asked Barak to raise an army, he agreed on one condition:

> *And Barak said unto her: "If thou wilt go*
> *with me, then I will go; but if thou wilt not*
> *go with me, I will not go."*

Barak was the strongest warrior of the time, but he would not enter the battlefield without the support and prayers of Deborah. Her reply?

> *"I will surely go with thee; notwithstanding*
> *the journey that thou takest shall not be for*
> *thy honor; for the Lord will give Sisera over*
> *into the hand of a woman."*

The army would fall, but General Sisera, King Jabin's commander in chief, would fall by the hands of a woman. One might assume this would be Deborah, but one would be assuming incorrectly.

* * *

Part II

YAEL WAS A CONTEMPORARY of Deborah's and another strong female figure of the time. Yael was identified as the wife of Heber the Kenite. Heber was known to have a peace treaty with King Jabin, who had been oppressing the Israelites for more than 20 years. So it would be natural that King Jabin's dwindled and retreating army would seek refuge from Heber's kin. And the defeated General Sisera, leader of King Jabin's army, ran to Yael and asked for shelter. She initially complied, offering him a place to rest and when Sisera mentioned his thirst and asked for water, Yael instead offered him some milk to drink.

While Barak's army and Deborah's prayer all but destroyed their enemies, it was Yael's ingenuity and bravery that brought down the mighty warrior Sisera, as previously prophesied by Deborah. You see, Yael gave the wicked general milk to tire him out, and when he fell into a deep slumber, she slew him with a tent peg. And when Barak went to find Sisera, Yael came out to meet him, and said: "Come, and I will show thee the man whom thou seekest. And he came unto her; and, behold, Sisera lay dead, and the tent-pin was in his temples."

Yael's bravery and cunning were such that her story was afforded a detailed description in the song of Deborah. In theory, Yael might have been seen as the enemy of the Jewish prophetess Deborah. Instead, Yael recognized the evil King Jabin and his oppressive regime and used her position to kill General Sisera. It's possible to imagine that a sort of sisterhood was formed that trumped earlier alliances and loyalties.

Stop Hiding Under a Cloud

HAVE YOU EVER TRIED TO GET through the fog of a really bad mood? It can be both overwhelming and incomprehensible to feel that blue, and worse, it can cause you to shut out the most important people in your life. Lamentations 3:8 says:

> Thou hast covered thyself with a cloud,
> so that no prayer can pass through.

Sometimes bad moods can start to feel so cozy that you wrap yourself in them like a blanket to keep the world away. What started out as righteous anger can become a self-righteous way of keeping life at bay. But giving in to a bad mood for the sake of sulking can also effectively block you from seeing or experiencing the really great things in life. Try to figure out a way past the blues when possible. Bad moods can be healthy at times, but when it feels more indulgent than necessary, try to remember what you might be missing.

Short Prayer for Healing

FEW THINGS INSPIRE A RETURN to prayer like the illness of a loved one. The feelings of helplessness, frustration, and terror combine and combust to create the urge to beg a higher power to listen and help. And despite the fact that there are prayers that go on for pages and eloquently express all these things, sometimes the urgency or inability to concentrate requires the expression of a pure burst of need.

Moses was a man of both deep faith and deep loyalty. And when faced with the illness of his sister Miriam—she was stricken with leprosy after saying unkind things about him—he cried out: *El Na Refa Na Lah* (Numbers 12:13). This is the shortest prayer in the Bible and translates to:

> *Heal her now, God, I beseech Thee.*

It wasn't considered disrespectful; it was to the point, and within seven days, Miriam had healed.

Note that the word *Lah* means her. If using this short prayer for a man, you may substitute the Hebrew word *Lo*.

I Won't Desert You

THE DEFINITION OF FRIENDSHIP and loyalty have changed significantly in the past few years. Friendship used to mean more than a peripheral acquaintance or online connection. Friendships could last lifetimes and through great adversity. These days, things can feel less solid. It can be hard to know who's a true friend, and who's only there on the surface. It's harder yet to know who will be there for you during both the best of times and the very worst ones.

Isaiah, especially 54:10, is full of incredible praise, but also the deepest words of loyalty and comfort.

> *For the mountains may depart, and*
> *the hills be removed; but my kindness*
> *shall not depart from you, neither shall*
> *my covenant of peace be removed, says*
> *the Lord who has compassion for you.*

It's a wonderful meditation on loyalty, continuity, and unwavering support. Even when you're not always sure of your friends, you can be sure of this.

The Blessing You Never Quite Expected

YOU KNOW THOSE SIGNS posted in public bathrooms everywhere—the ones stating that employees must wash hands before returning to work? Well, here's something unexpected: observant Jews not only wash their hands after using the restroom, they recite a blessing as well.

Fourth-century Babylonian Talmudic sage Abayei composed a blessing called *Asher Yatzar*, which translated means "(He) Who Formed Mankind." It's an interesting blessing because it deals with the most basic function, and can seem slightly graphic as it mentions one's "orifices and cavities." The blessing then refers to said cavities, saying that, "If one of them were to be ruptured or one of them to be blocked, it would be impossible for a person to survive."

If you've ever had a loved one affected by kidney issues or digestive diseases, you'll know just how disruptive to a day-to-day existence it can be. This blessing that's recited numerous times daily reminds people never to take their bodily functions for granted.

Blessing on Bread

WHILE THERE ARE MANY blessings made over different foods, the blessing on bread is slightly different. A meal that starts with or includes bread, even if it's a snack, is considered a full meal. For that reason, it's customary to start the meal by not only washing one's hands (and reciting the proper blessing afterward) but also by making a separate blessing over the bread itself. And when eating a full meal, it isn't necessary to make any additional blessings over foods eaten.

The crux of the *Hamotzei* blessing is *Hamotzei lechem min ha'aretz*:

> *Who brings forth bread from the earth*

It's a lovely way of acknowledging not only the finished product, but the process that gave us wheat to make into bread.

Sometimes the Answer Is No

THERE ARE SEVERAL PLACES throughout the book of Exodus where God says to Moses some variation of:

I will harden Pharaoh's heart.

Not that Pharaoh will be stubborn or obnoxious or just mean, but that there will be a higher power controlling Pharaoh's movements, if not his ability to make choices and decisions. Moses might beseech Pharaoh and beg for freedom for the Jews enslaved in Egypt, but the answer will always be, "No." And this course of action will lead to a previously unforeseen series of events and outcomes.

Issues of free will aside, it's an interesting notion to explore. People of faith can hope and pray and wish, but sometimes there will be things that remain elusive or unattainable. And it's impossible to gauge or even try to guess the reasons. When prayers feel ignored it can be tempting to lose faith.

Sometimes there are variables that we will never understand. And sometimes, despite one's best efforts, the answer will still be, "No." That doesn't mean that you should stop asking. It just means that you didn't get the hoped for answer this time around.

Perek Shira:
The Song of Creation

Introduction

MY FATHER IS ONE OF the most brilliant and learned people that I know, almost eerily so. He denies having a photographic memory, but if you ask him a question on even the most arcane topic, you can almost see him turning the pages in his mind until he gets to the tract or quotation he's been looking for. And I wish you could have seen his face light up when he mentioned *Perek Shira* to me for the first time.

Though some say it was composed by King David, *Perek Shira*, which translates literally to "Chapter of Song" but is more often referred to as the Song of Creation, isn't attributed to one author but rather seems to borrow heavily from different elements of biblical tracts.

I was intrigued by the notion of a single prayer that highlights all prayers said to be uttered on a daily basis by all the creatures and beings of the universe. It includes 84 elements and everything from earth to lions to insects, and like Aesop's fables, it is considered by some to be a parable for the character-

istics to which people should aspire. Since it's such an incredibly robust prayer, I'll include numerous excerpts from *Perek Shira* throughout this book.

Chapter 2 goes through the day, the night, the sun, and moon, and by 2:6 (which originates in Psalms 18:12) gets to the darkest clouds. The Thick Clouds are saying:

> *He made darkness His secret place;*
> *His pavilion around Him was dark*
> *with waters and thick clouds of the skies.*

There are so many metaphors about dark clouds and silver linings. Maybe there's another way to look at it too. Maybe the clouds are there sometimes just to offer some respite from everything else. Sometimes it's important to take a step back and just be, before you can go on with everything else in your life.

The Trees

*P*EREK *SHIRA* IS CALLED the Song of Creation because it includes prayers for all elements and creatures on earth. *Perek Shira* 3:1 includes this passage, originally found in Chronicles I, 16:33:

> *The Trees of the Field say:*
> *"Then shall the trees of the forest sing*
> *out at the presence of the Lord,*
> *for He comes to judge the earth."*

When I was a little girl, I learned that every living thing on earth prays in the way that is native to it. So, a dramatic looking weeping willow wasn't in fact weeping, but rather offering praise. And in some way, and to this day, whenever I pass a tree with its branches gently swaying in the wind, I smile to myself and think that it's praying in a way that only a tree can.

Sometimes the words aren't there, but the intentions or emotions can be.

Lift Your Voice

A LOT OF THE PROPHECIES of Isaiah are seen as being dire and full of warnings and rebuke. And while I try not to take words and thoughts out of context, sometimes there are lessons to be learned and inspiration to be had even in warnings. Chapter 58 in Isaiah begins:

> *Cry aloud, spare not,*
> *lift up thy voice like a horn.*

Unlike Psalm 98, which encourages you to "make a joyful noise," this is more in the context of praying after a transgression—finding your voice again after losing a bit of yourself. That said, sometimes when things feel wrong, you need to talk about it, scream about it, and yell until you feel better or can make things better.

Wake Up:
Accomplish Things!

ONE OF THE CHAPTERS in *Perek Shira*, the Song of Creation, that feels most like a children's story or maybe like the wisdom of Benjamin Franklin, is Chapter 4, which is all about the rooster. The chapter goes through the rooster's calls, from first to last, and includes bits of wisdom for those inclined to laziness. In its fifth call the rooster says:

> *How long will you recline, Oh lazy one?*
> *When will you rise from your sleep?*
> *(Proverbs 6:9)*

In its sixth call the rooster says:

> *Do not love sleep, or you will grow poor;*
> *open your eyes and you shall be satiated with*
> *bread. (Proverbs 20:13)*

While most of us use alarm clocks to wake up, the wisdom of the rooster is pretty universal: get up, stay up, and you'll earn a living and/or enjoy a delicious breakfast!

Build a Solid Foundation

I CAN'T BEGIN TO TELL YOU just how many times my mother said to me growing up, "A lazy person works twice." It's true, though. If you don't do something right the first time around, chances are that you'll just have to start over again. What about when you're building your network of friends? Your family? A career? Well, it's kind of the same thing. If you're not doing things the right way, chances are you'll have to start over again or will always be trying to fix something that just isn't right. In Psalm 11:3 King David says:

When the foundations are destroyed,
what hath the righteous wrought?

It's hard to make things right when they just weren't right to begin with. Try to take a step back and set strong foundations for your life and especially in relationships before continuing to build toward the next level.

Rise Above

*P*EREK *S*HIRA, THE SONG OF CREATION, includes snippets of prayers that all of the creatures and elements in nature might utter. While most of those snippets have different origins, they're united in this single prayer to present a holistic worldview. What if every single element in nature had a song to personify or anthropomorphize it?

When one pictures an eagle, one likely pictures a strong and majestic creature soaring above everything else. And who among us wouldn't like to be like the eagle, impervious to life's little barbs and setbacks? In *Perek Shira*, the Eagle says these words originally found in Psalms 59:6:

> *And You, God, Lord of Hosts, Lord*
> *of Israel, arouse to punish the nations;*
> *do not pardon the wicked traitors, Selah.*

It isn't easy to turn off your anxiety or fear or despair in every situation. Sometimes though, it might just be the best thing to channel an eagle and realize that you can't fight and win every single time. Sometimes, you just have to rise above.

On Embarrassing Others

PSALM 83 IS PRETTY INTENSE and includes a litany of many ancient battles fought and victories or defeats along the way. And the psalmist asks God for help defeating his enemies in very creative ways, at one point saying that a former enemy became "as the dung of the earth." Well, that's a pretty descriptive and very appropriate end for an enemy. What struck me, though, were Verses 17–18, where the psalmist asks that God humiliate his enemies in many different ways:

> *Fill their faces with shame...Let them*
> *be ashamed and affrighted for ever;*
> *yea, let them be abashed and perish.*

Doesn't mere humiliation seem far too good for an enemy? Not quite. It's been said by the sages that humiliating someone is akin to causing their death, sometimes because they lose social standing and become nonentities in their former worlds. It's a good lesson to really think before saying something that might embarrass someone else—even if you think they deserve it.

Home/Loyalty

*P*EREK *SHIRA*, THE SONG OF CREATION, contains many wonderful bits of prayer attributed to different creatures and elements. I'd like to group two together for some thoughts on loyalty and home. In Chapter 4:13, part of what the songbird says is originally found in Psalms 84:4:

> *A bird has also found its home and*
> *the sparrow a nest for herself where*
> *she placed her young*

The chapter that immediately follows 4:14 is for the swallow, a bird whose symbolism I've always loved. It contains this passage originally found in Psalms 30:13:

> *The Swallow says: "So that my soul shall*
> *sing your honor and shall not be silent, my*
> *God—I shall forever thank you."*

If you pair these prayers, there are so many elements of safety and nesting, home and family, loyalty and return. Many people use the expression "nesting," to describe that cozy blissful feeling of being part of a warm and loving unit. The swallow, on the other hand, generally represents a wanderer who always returns home again.

The Golden Rule

NEAR THE BEGINNING of the daily prayer service, it's common to include this phrase from Leviticus 19:18:

Love your neighbor as yourself.

Some variation of that theme is found in nearly every faith and religion from Bahaism to Wicca, leading one to believe that it really is an excellent mantra to begin one's day. Our culture boasts the greatest innovations known to man, along with modern maladies ranging from road rage to online flame wars. And the safety of one's car or online anonymity shouldn't preclude universal good manners and etiquette. Take a step back from a situation and put yourself on the receiving end of that next harangue. Or stop ignoring or vaguely gesticulating to the person at the newsstand or to the bank teller or salesperson in favor of continuing your phone conversation. Modern technology shouldn't trump old-fashioned manners.

The Fruits of Your Labors

IN *PEREK SHIRA*, THE SONG OF CREATION, even the Beast of Burden is given its own special chapter. In Chapter 5:4, the Beast of Burden says these words, originally found in Psalms 128:2:

> *When you eat the fruit of your labors, you are happy and satisfied with your lot.*

A few years back I planted soybeans in small pots scattered throughout my matchbox-size kitchen. I can't begin to describe my rapturous joy when those things started growing and the vines twined around my kitchen window. My entire "crop" amounted to about 16 soybean pods total, but I boiled them and salted them and served them to my perplexed guests who could not understand my giddiness at their enjoying my microscopic offerings.

Work isn't fun and it's rarely easy. But when you've finished a presentation or painted the garage or iced a cake, there's an incredible feeling of satisfaction unmatched to the store-bought variety. Doesn't it feel great when your hard work pays off?

Pitzi's Prayer

IN *PEREK SHIRA*, THE SONG OF CREATION, most of the birds and beasts in all of creation have a short chapter dedicated just to them—man's best friend being no exception. In fact there are two chapters dedicated to dogs, one to hounds (some say this chapter is about a specific kind of dog, an outdoor dog or greyhound). Chapter 5:17 of *Perek Shira* is dedicated to the humble dog. The hound uses these words, originally found in Psalms 33:1:

> *Let the righteous rejoice in God,*
> *praise befits the straight ones.*

It's hard to imagine a creature more straightforward than a dog, which is known for incredible loyalty. People could learn a thing or two from the loyalty of dogs.

If you'll indulge me for a moment, I'd like to share a story about Pitzi*, who in my opinion is one of the most loyal dogs in history. In 1943, when my Hungarian-born father was 11 years old, he and his entire family, and most of the Jews in Hungary, were rounded up by the Nazis and sent to a series of labor camps, concentration camps, and death camps in Germany. My father's pet dog, Pitzi, was left home to fend for himself. Nearly two years passed, during which time millions of Jews were murdered by the Nazis. Though my father and both of his parents survived, most of their family (and my mother's as well) perished in the camps.

Some time after the liberation, my father and his family were finally allowed to return home. They were greeted with boos and death threats at the railroad stations; angry neighbors tried to scare off the survivors who were home to reclaim their property. As my father alighted from the train he was greeted by raucous barking. His beloved Pitzi was there waiting for him at the station, eager to welcome him home.

In a time when the entire world had confused wrong with right, one pet dog made all the difference in the world to a young boy who had been to hell and back.

---

*An affectionate Hungarian word meaning small. Pitzi the dog was a great giant of a beast.

Seek Justice

IN *PEREK SHIRA*, THE SONG OF CREATION, it's interesting to note that the wolf, who in fairy tales and fables has a reputation as being the bad guy, is the one to warn people against taking the law into their own hands. In Chapter 5:13 the Wolf says these words, originally found in Exodus 22:8:

> *For every matter of trespass, whether it*
> *be for ox, for ass, for sheep, for clothing,*
> *or any lost thing, for which he says: "This*
> *is it," the cause of both parties shall come*
> *before God; he whom God shall condemn*
> *shall pay double unto his neighbor.*

Don't be a wolf in sheep's clothing. Don't try to prove that you're right when you've already been proven wrong, because in the end, truth will out.

The Pursuit of Justice

FOR ME, THIS PARTICULAR SAYING from Deuter-onomy 16:20 is more of a mantra than a prayer. *Tzedek, Tzedek Tirdof*, translates to:

> *Justice, justice shall you pursue.*

This is a bit tricky to understand. For thousands of years, scholars have wondered why the word "justice" is repeated. In prayers and in biblical texts, a word repeated has special significance. In this case, it means that not only should you pursue justice, but you should also be mindful of the way in which you pursue it. Chase justice in a just way. Don't cut corners or allow untruths to cloud your pursuit of the right thing.

Tzedek, Tzedek Tirdof is also known as the Lawyer's Creed, so that attorneys will be mindful of the ways in which they chase claims and successful outcomes. Lawyers are a much-maligned group, but without their power to use words to protect their clients, we'd all be scrambling for our own forms of justice.

And while you're at it, don't wait for a lawyer or person in a position of power to pursue justice for you. It isn't easy to do the right thing, but speaking up about even small injustices can be a personal form of pursuing justice in the right way.

Cat and Mouse

CAT LOVERS REJOICE! There is a prayer just for cats in *Perek Shira*. In Chapter 5:18, these words originally found in Psalms 30:2 celebrate the fiercer aspects of our feline friends. The Cat says:

I shall pursue my enemies and overtake them, and I shall not return until they are destroyed.

If you've ever watched a cat determined to catch a mouse, this prayer will resonate with you. There's no shame in pursuing or wanting to be rid of your natural enemies. While everyone's ideal is a peaceful co-existence, if someone repeatedly does the wrong thing to you and yours, you have a moral obligation to make sure that they're brought to justice. It doesn't make you petty or vindictive or someone who holds a grudge; it makes you someone committed to ensuring that a bad person does not continue to prey on others.

The Industrious Ant

IN *PEREK SHIRA*, THE SONG OF CREATION, the Ant's Prayer, originally found in Proverbs 6:6, is a tiny chapter near the end. The Ant says:

> *Go to the ant, sluggard;*
> *consider its ways and become wise.*

It's hard to walk outdoors in the springtime or summer without seeing ants milling about in huge clusters and doing incredible amounts of work. And it's hard not to be inspired to be more productive when faced with the sheer might of the entire ant colony working together for their greater good.

In the corporate and working world, people tend to bandy about really tired expressions, including the old chestnut, "There's no 'I' in team," or some such not so inspirational idiom. It can be hard to be a team member when all you really want to do is soar on your own, but there are many occasions in life when you have to work as a member of a group for the greater good.

Blessing on a Rainbow

UNLIKE MOST CULTURES and faiths that delight in the sight of a rainbow, observant Jews tend to feel uneasy when seeing a prism across the sky. For them, a rainbow represents a warning of sorts. After the great flood, when Noah and his family emerged from the ark, God showed them a rainbow as visual proof that he'd never again flood the earth and destroy most of its beings. Genesis 9:13 states, "I (God) have set a rainbow in the cloud, and it shall be a sign of the covenant between Me and the earth." For that reason these words are said when seeing a rainbow:

Who remembers His covenant, is trustworthy
in His covenant, and fulfills His word.

We're secure that there will never be another great and destructive flood, but natural disasters can remind us just how fragile our individual worlds and environments can be.

Blessing on Thunder

I DON'T KNOW ABOUT YOU, but I love a good thunderstorm, most especially when I don't have to go anywhere and can stay indoors and—better yet—tucked under the covers with a good book. There's actually a blessing said when hearing thunder:

Blessed are you Lord, our God,
king of the universe, whose power
and might fill the world.

For those who find thunderstorms scary, it's a comforting way of reassuring oneself that even a thunderstorm might be part of a higher power. I wonder if there's also a great object lesson there: sometimes the things that seem really scary can be the ones that eventually lead us to a greater place of calm. Is there anything that scares you but also ultimately ends up bringing you a renewed sense of peace?

The Song of the Lion

P OP CULTURE IS FULL of references to lions—
everything from the Cowardly Lion in *The
Wizard of Oz*, to Simba in *The Lion King*. What's
interesting about the reference to the lion in *Perek
Shira*, the Song of Creation, is the way that the lion
ostensibly offers its most notable characteristics to
God—along with those of the fiercest and mighti-
est of men. In *Perek Shira* 5:13, The Lion says,

> *God shall go forth as a mighty man;*
> *as a warrior arouses zeal, He shall shout,*
> *even roar; He shall overcome His enemies.*

Many say that ancient poetry, liturgy, prayer, and
song shouldn't be taken literally, that instead it's
been written so that people could have imagery
that they understand to encompass a greater power. In this case, though, it's empowering to think
that both a lion and his God are influenced by
the characteristics of the bravest of men. In other
words, look everywhere for inspiration and learn
to roar or shout when necessary.

Blessings After Nourishment

Part I

FOLLOWING A COMPLETE MEAL that includes bread, it's customary to recite the *Birkat Hamazon*, a rather lengthy and lovely prayer thanking God for the food and other blessings received. The prayer is made up of four initial blessings followed by additional praise and thanks. On holidays, additional sections are added.

The prayer is read quietly and to oneself on weekdays and sung as a group (or at least parts of it are) on special occasions such as weddings and holidays. The instructions are in Deuteronomy 8:10: "When you have eaten and are satisfied, you shall bless the Lord your God for the good land which He gave you." While saying grace in advance of a meal can prepare you for the bounty you are about to enjoy, *Birkat Hamazon* allows you to muse and be grateful for the delicious feast you've just enjoyed. The first blessing begins:

> *Blessed are you, Lord our God, king of the universe, who, in his goodness, provides sustenance for the entire world with grace, with kindness, and with mercy.*

There are those who might feel this prayer is a bit disingenuous, seeing as there is so much poverty and famine in the world. It's important to remember that prayers such as this one are meant to offer praise. In this case, wanting to extend the joy of your own bounty with others.

* * *

Part II

ONE OF MY FAVORITE PARTS of the *Birkat Hamazon* is a short exhortation:

May the merciful one provide our livelihood with honor.

Every single time I read it, I think anew about the brilliant simplicity of that simple line.

We've all been through incredibly trying times at one point or another in our lives. It feels like the entire country has been struggling over the past few years. And if we haven't been affected personally by the painfully sluggish economy, we have friends or loved ones who are struggling to make ends meet. When thanking a greater power for our wonderful bounty, we sometimes might wonder where our next meal might come from. And we hope that we'll be able to support ourselves with grace and honor and pride. It also can double as a mantra before a job interview.

Part III

THE BLESSINGS AFTER FOOD offer so many great life lessons. For instance, as children we take it for granted that we'll be fed, clothed, and cared for by the adults in our lives. After putting their children first in all things, parents can definitely feel unappreciated and completely taken for granted. There's a passage in the grace after meals in which we recognize and acknowledge the many roles that our parents play in our lives:

> *May the merciful one bless my father,*
> *my teacher, the master of this house,*
> *and my mother, my teacher, the mistress*
> *of this house; them, their household,*
> *their children, and all that is theirs;*
> *us, and all that is ours.*

It's a great thing to remind children not to take things for granted and to acknowledge and thank those that care for them.

Blessing for Lightning or Unusual Occurrences in Nature

DID YOU EVER GET really freaked out when sitting through a particularly intense lightning storm? There's actually a blessing to be said on lightning:

Blessed are You, God, our Lord, king of the universe, who reenacts the work of creation.

It's a pretty nifty blessing because it refers to the very acts of creation, which must have presented quite a spectacle. The same blessing can also be said upon seeing a shooting star or comet, or being in the middle of an earthquake. At the very least, it's a way to distract oneself from worrying about the storm.

As children many of us were taught to count the seconds between each flash of lightning and each crash of thunder. Perhaps this is a great lesson to help us deal with crises as well. Concentrate on what's most important and figure out the rest when things calm down a bit.

There's Hope for Everyone

SNAKES HAVE A REALLY BAD REPUTATION. The original snake was blamed for enticing Adam and Eve to eat the forbidden fruit, and when someone's pretty horrible we call that person a snake. In *Perek Shira*, the Song of Creation, even the slithering snake has a prayer. In Chapter 6:3 the Snake says these words, originally found in Psalms 145:14:

> *God supports the fallen and*
> *straightens the bent.*

There's one school of thought that would suggest that the lowly snake can't help itself for being that way, and that a person who reminds you of a snake is just following his or her true nature. After looking at the short prayer for a snake, though, it gives one hope that even someone who's spent their lives on a crooked path can find their way back.

The Tofu of Blessings

THERE'S A COMPLICATED collection of blessings that are made before eating certain foods and different ones to coincide afterward. One of the few blessings that is something of a catch-all is *Shehakol*: everything. If you're drinking juice or having a candy, you can recite the *Shehakol* blessing. If you're unsure of what to say or just want to snack on something, you can recite *Shehakol*. I like to think of it as the tofu of blessings; it takes on almost all flavors and textures as its own.

Meanwhile, grammar nerds might take issue with the verbiage because it starts off by talking directly to God and then changes into a description of his prowess.

> *Blessed are You, Lord, our God,*
> *king of the universe, everything*
> *was created through His words.*

I like to think of it as being awestruck by just how much He can do—either that, or acknowledging that some things can't be labeled, and rather than list them as being one-size-fits-all, it's a lot nicer to praise their creator.

The Psalms of King David

KING DAVID WAS A LARGER-THAN-LIFE figure of the Bible. An incredibly complex man, he was revered as much for his incredible knowledge and love of learning as for the ways he was betrayed and persecuted by those closest to him. Symbolically, he is associated with his harp/violin and with the six-pointed star known as the Star of David.

David was also the poet, primary composer, and sometimes editor of the Book of Psalms. The word "Psalm" originated from the Greek word *psalmoi*, which means "music of the lyre" or "songs sung to a harp," because some say that David composed these beautiful poems to accompany music played on his stringed instrument. In Hebrew, the word for Psalms is *Tehillim*. *Tehila* means "praise" in Hebrew, so the plural for *Tehillim* means "praises."

The Psalms reflect on the different life stages of David. They also teach how best to act in both wonderful or awful moments. Some of the Psalms are prayers, some advice; and for countless people, the Psalms offer tremendous courage and inspiration.

The chapters of the Psalms can be broken down into daily portions to be completed on a weekly or monthly basis, depending on personal preference.

Psalms Introduction

BECAUSE THERE ARE 150 very potent chapters in the Book of Psalms, I have included a large proportion of Psalms and inspirational quotes or sections contained within.

And speaking of inspirational, I'm in awe of my mother. She's elegant and stylish, but more than that, she's modest to a fault about all of the good things that she does for others. Among other things, my mom regularly shops for groceries and cooks delicious meals for those in her community facing some sort of adversity or illness in their families. My mother also keeps a list of people who are gravely ill and says Psalms for them daily. She's a powerhouse of positive thought, even during the darkest times, and she's had her share of really bad days.

When I was diagnosed with late-stage cancer, my mother never crumbled—not in front of me, at least. And when I went through six months of chemo and countless surgeries, she never once slacked off on saying her Psalms daily. When I was in the infusion room at the hospital being systematically poisoned by a blend of four types of chemo meant to cure me, and when I was weak and angry and felt that I'd been abandoned by a God I once felt so close to, I knew

that all I had to do was look up and see my mother's head bent over her Book of Psalms. Because her faith was unflagging and because she never stopped believing in the power of her prayers, I had to believe as well. My mother is a force of nature, and she intended her prayers to count. And I believe with all of my heart that they do.

While I have many thoughts on Psalms, I always think first and foremost of my mother and her daily commitment to saying each day's portion. And when I asked her for her favorite, she gets slightly misty-eyed as she recites by heart Chapter 128, A Song of Ascents.

Prayer for the Sick Before Saying Psalms

IF YOU VISIT ANY social-networking websites or message boards, you'll likely see people requesting prayers or good thoughts sent their way, or to someone in dire circumstances or poor health. There's also a lovely custom of circulating prayer lists for those who might be in need of extra prayers.

In the case of ancient prayers being used in modern times, it's traditional before saying the Psalms to say a short prayer including each ill person's first name and that of his or her mother.

One of the more sobering moments of my life was when close friends aware of my cancer diagnosis asked for my full name, so that they could add me to their prayer list. I'm not sure that I can effectively convey what that meant to me. I'd always heard people mention those in need of extra prayers, but at that moment, I was the person desperate for any help. It was perhaps one of the lowest points of my entire life. And I've had quite a few.

Now that I'm fully in remission (surreptitiously knocks on wood), I send up an extra prayer of thanks every time I receive a request to pray for someone who is ill.

Before saying Psalms, it's customary to recite the following short prayer and insert the name or names of the ill in the form of FIRST NAME daughter/son of MOTHER'S FIRST NAME.

May it be your will, my God and
God of my fathers, that in the merit
of saying these songs of Psalms,
you will send complete recovery
quickly from the heavens, healing of
the soul and physical healing, for the sick
[say the name or names of the sick here]
among the remainder of the sick of Israel.

Don't worry if you don't actually know your friend's correct name or that of his or her mother. It's the good thought and intentions that count most in this case.

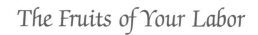

The Fruits of Your Labor

WE ALL HAVE DIFFERENT working styles. Some of us thrive most in a bustling work space, bouncing ideas and inspiration off of colleagues. Others prefer to lock ourselves in a room and toil continuously until a project is completed. Our personal styles can be radically different as well. In Psalm 128:2, the psalmist says:

> When thou eatest the labour of
> thy hands, happy shalt thou be,
> and it shall be well with thee.

The Psalm discusses generations of a happy and flourishing family life, but the commenters refer to professional accomplishments. The common thread, though, is the satisfaction of living to see your hard work and accomplishments bear fruit.

Know Your Truth/
Do Your Best

Prayer isn't always uplifting or beautiful or poetic. Sometimes it's raw and desperate. And sometimes it's important to reflect on the fact that we're only human, and as such, have to acknowledge and appreciate our own limitations, but that doesn't mean that we don't have to try.

When King Hezekiah was very ill, the prophet Isaiah came to him and told him to set his house in order. And Hezekiah wept mightily and prayed. Part of his prayer included these words from Kings 2:20:

Remember now, Oh Lord, I beseech thee,
how I have walked before thee in truth and
with a whole heart, and have done that
which is good in thy sight.

It can be incredibly difficult to stay true to one's own values and ethics in a morally complex world. Sometimes the simplest way to resist some of the more noxious elements of our fast-paced world is to trust your own moral compass. Know your truth. Even if you slip up every now and again, your heart won't let you lie to yourself.

Everything in Its Time

I ASKED MY SISTER KIKI what her favorite prayer or chapter of verse was, and was a little surprised when she told me that it was part of the first chapter of the Psalms. I reread the text and realized that when I read the original text in Hebrew and then translations in English, I usually came away with two entirely different experiences. Though I grew up hearing Hebrew spoken in my home along with other languages, and attended bilingual schools from kindergarten through high school, Hebrew is still not my first language. This means that, while I can skim through English text, I'll usually pay closer attention to the Hebrew texts in the hopes of better understanding the spirit of the words, along with the literal translation.

In rereading Chapter 1:3, I was amazed that while I was familiar with this verse, I missed it in search of the larger translation. Kiki's favorite part is:

> *And he shall be like a tree planted*
> *by streams of water, that brings*
> *forth its fruit in its season, and*
> *whose leaf does not wither; and in*
> *whatsoever he does he shall succeed.*

My sister and I have had many conversations over the years about the notion of early bloomers and late bloomers and everything in between. What she liked best about this particular verse was the notion that the idealized person described here is compared to a tree that blossoms in the time that is exactly right for that tree—not before, not after, but at the moment perfect for him alone. There's so much societal pressure to be something that you aren't, at perhaps a time that isn't right for you. In a perfect world, we'd all bloom at the exact moment that was right for us alone.

Alienated Family Members

AT SOME POINT OR ANOTHER, in almost every family, a rift develops, and two family members stop speaking to each other. What may have started as an argument becomes a veritable feud. Tolstoy famously said, "Happy families are all alike; every unhappy family is unhappy in its own way." Historically, that feels entirely true. In the case of King David, Psalms 3:1 shows his despair at being pursued by his own son:

> A Psalm of David, when he fled
> from Absalom his son. Lord, how
> many are mine adversaries become!
> Many are they that rise up against me.

Even the great King David was completely vulnerable when running away from his own son. His despair is evident throughout much of the Book of Psalms. Sometimes families fall apart and just can't be mended, no matter how hard you try. Other times, it simply takes years and effort.

One of my favorite biblical theories involves Jacob and his son Joseph. According to the stories, at age 17 Joseph, the favorite son of Jacob, was sold into slavery in Egypt by his envious brothers. Nearly two decades passed before Jacob and his beloved son were once again reunited. Fathers and sons and mothers and daughters lock horns and have a hard time seeing eye-to-eye—usually from the time that they hit their teens until they're in their thirties and start to appreciate what a hard time their own parents had.

Avoid Bad Influences

FRIENDSHIP IS A pretty complicated thing. Sure, everyone wants exciting and interesting friends, but who wasn't told as a child to avoid friends who were bad influences? And it's almost cliché, the way some women gravitate toward bad boys and then end up miserable. The first words in the Book of Psalms seem a fitting bit of wisdom to impart:

> *Happy is the man that hath not walked*
> *in the counsel of the wicked, nor stood*
> *in the way of sinners, nor sat in*
> *the seat of the scornful.*

Life is hard enough without giving into peer pressure—at any age. Moreover, if you avoid negative influences, it's easier to remain positive about your own life and outlook.

Fight Authority
(When Appropriate!)

In Psalms, Chapter 2, there's a lot of discussion of wrongdoing. This part, in Psalms 2:10, struck me:

> *Now therefore, Oh ye kings, be wise; be admonished, ye judges of the earth.*

We read on a daily basis about politicians and CEOs involved in scandals or corrupt behavior. It's almost a given that those voted into office will at some point serve their egos or selves before serving the needs of their constituents. The thing is, if a leader doesn't serve the best interests of the people, it's important to voice displeasure. Even in a work setting, if your boss is unethical or not doing the best thing by your company or colleagues, try to figure out a way to discuss the issue instead of standing by as things get worse. Unions would never have been started if the workers had not united to create more fair work environments.

Trust in a Higher Power

THE FINAL VERSE in Psalms, Chapter 3 is comforting in that it allows you to realize that sometimes not everything is up to you. Be it divine power or the universe or karma, not everything in life is in your control.

Salvation belongeth unto the Lord;
Thy blessing be upon thy people.

Worrying won't change things. Sure, it's important to have a Plan A, and sometimes a Plan B. Heck, throw in a Plan C if that calms your mind some. And plan and strategize and figure out how to get through and work toward a better day. But in some circumstances, the only thing that you can do is let go of your own need to control everything and just trust in above.

Tremble Not

PSALM 4 INCLUDES a lovely excerpt that many people say as part of their nightly prayers. I'll include both the transliterated Hebrew and the English version:

Rigzu ve'al tech'tau, imru bilvavchem
Al Mishkavchem, Vidomu Selah

Tremble, and sin not; commune with your
own heart upon your bed, and be still.
Selah.

There are many discussions about what the word *selah* means. Most say that it's simply an ancient word used in poems, verse, or song. I prefer the description that says it's a word meaning, "You must stop and listen to advice." Most people aren't afraid of the bogeyman during the day. It's at night when the world is dark and we're alone with our thoughts that things can get scary. This verse advises us to commune with our own hearts and simply be still: a lovely way to keep the nightmares at bay.

Hoisted by Their Own Petard

SOMETIMES IT CAN BE HARD to put your finger on just what bothers you about someone. Is the person so well versed in little white lies that he's all but forgotten how to tell the truth? Maybe she's so busy bragging about how much she has that it's hard to see past her designer labels and remember the person that you used to like.

Psalm 5 can feel like a rant against the phony or more dangerous people so many of us can face. King David discusses how hard he tries to do the right thing, how so many insist or persist in lying and wrongdoing. He then asks God to protect him from just those people. It's a fairly short chapter that expresses his frustration and fears.

> *Oh Lord, lead me in thy righteousness*
> *because of them that lie in wait for me;*
> *make Thy way straight before my face.*

He also includes some pretty amazing imagery, comparing the mouths of these people to a yawning grave. Best yet, toward the end, King David includes a zinger:

> *Hold them guilty, O God,*
> *let them fall by their own counsels.*

The Boomerang Prayer

IN PSALM 6, David is in pain. He discusses not just the physical pain, but also the internal turmoil he's going through: "My soul also is sore affrighted." It's a painful chapter where David relates just how hard every day is for him. But after his deep despair, things turn around for David:

> Depart from me, all ye workers of iniquity;
>   for the Lord hath heard the voice of
>   my weeping. The Lord hath heard my
>   supplication; the Lord receiveth my prayer.

It becomes sort of a turning point; David hasn't been weeping out of weakness, but rather from frustration, and once his cries have been heard, his attitude and requests change:

> All mine enemies shall be ashamed and
>   sore affrighted; they shall turn back,
>   they shall be ashamed suddenly.

It's a marvelous moment where David turns the shame and pain inflicted on him by his enemies and sends it right back to them. A moment of weakness turned to strength. You can't always control the painful or cruel things that others say to you, but you can realize that perhaps it is they who should be the ones ashamed of their behavior and cruelty.

More Karma

THERE ARE MANY RECURRING THEMES in the Book of Psalms: running from one's enemies, seeking salvation, and seeing your enemies all receive their just desserts. In Psalm 7, King David says several times and in several different ways that those who seek to do evil to him will actually be hastening their own unfortunate endings. One example he offers is in 7:16:

> *He dug a pit, and hollowed it, and now has*
> *fallen into the ditch which he made …*
> *His mischief shall return upon his*
> *own head, and his violence shall*
> *come down upon his own pate.*

The idea of an evil or mischievous person bringing about his own downfall is one shared by many religions and cultures. Indian or Buddhist religions suggest there is a karmic wheel that can be set in motion by one's actions. For good or bad, our own actions beget positive or negative results.

Speak Yourself Confident

A LTHOUGH THE BOOK OF PROVERBS isn't techni-cally made up of prayers, the phrasing is both lyrical and offers timeless advice about how to conduct yourself when speaking or praying. In Proverbs 8:6, King Solomon says:

> *Hear, for I will speak excellent things, and*
> *the opening of my lips shall be right things.*

I feel like everyone should say this to themselves every morning before heading out to the office. We all want to say the right thing every time, but realistically, when put on the spot, sometimes the wrong words come out instead. Perhaps this is a nice way of also taking a mental break before blurting out impassioned words. And who are we kidding? Prayer is such a handy way of always having the right words to say at the right time.

Blessing on Wine
(And Even Grape Juice!)

THERE ARE NUMEROUS BLESSINGS for every type of food or drink on earth. And while most fruit juices, from apple to tangerine (that's as close to a fruit starting with a "Z" as I could think of), share the same blessing, grape juice has one of its own.

Blessed are you, Lord our God, ruler of the universe, who creates the fruit of the vine.

Because wine is used in so many rituals and on so many special occasions, it's given its own unique blessing. And believe it or not, grape juice falls into the same blessing category as wine does. I'm not much of an imbiber, but I do almost envy the ritual that many people have of ending their day with a lovely glass of wine. Do you have any daily rituals that allow you to take time away from everything else and everyone else and just reconnect with yourself or your partner?

Blessing on Fruit

THE BLESSING SAID OVER FRUIT is a pretty simple one:

Blessed are you, Lord, our God, king of the universe, who creates the fruit of the tree.

It's kind of nice to remind us that apples and oranges grow on trees and not in grocery aisles! It's also a pretty modest blessing, considering the sheer beauty and complexity of design and delivery system of fruit—citrus with the millions of tiny juice ampules contained within; pomegranates, with their gorgeous ruby-like seeds; or the sheer beauty of strawberries and kiwis. They're all so wonderful; it feels as though each deserves specific praise.

There's a custom on Rosh Hashanah, the Jewish New Year, to eat a new fruit (one that you haven't eaten for at least a year) or an exotic fruit. At that point, the *Shehecheyanu* blessing is also made.

Friday Night Blessing over Children

I'D ALWAYS GET ALL TEARY-EYED when I saw the scene in the movie *Fiddler on the Roof* where Tevye blesses his daughters on Friday night. I'm not sure why this wasn't a tradition in my household growing up, but it's such a meaningful thing for the head of household to take a moment to bless his children.

For a boy:

> *May God inspire you to live like*
> *Ephraim and Menasheh.*

For a girl:

> *May God inspire you to live like Sarah,*
> *Rebecca, Rachel, and Leah.*

Then for both or all children:

> *May God bless you and keep you.*

> *May God's light shine upon you,*
> *and may God be gracious to you.*

> *May you feel God's presence within*
> *you always, and may you find peace.*

Protection Against Enemies

WHEN WE FIRST THINK about ancient prayer or poetry, we likely think about songs of praise or even beseeching words, but a recurring theme throughout the Psalms is David's begging God to vanquish his enemies.

In modern times, and in our mostly civilized world, our enemies are often better disguised than "bad guys" are in the Bible. Sometimes your enemy is a friend who's not actually that friendly, or an energy vampire who wants to suck the life and optimism out of you. For those times, it's helpful to think about the big picture and what you truly want out of your relationships.

And sometimes, the problem with an enemy is bigger than that. There's someone who truly wishes you or your loved ones harm. If there's no superhero around to intervene, it's comforting to muse on these more aggressive words found in Psalms 9:20:

> *Set terror over them (my enemies) Oh Lord;*
> *let the nations know they are but men.*

Prayer doesn't have to be all lightness all of the time. Sometimes it helps to feel empowered and to get even your angriest thoughts out in words.

Sometimes You Feel All Alone in the World

I T ISN'T ALWAYS LOGICAL, and it doesn't always have to make sense: You can have a large, loving, boisterous family, an extended network of friends, and you may live in the most crowded city in the world, but you still may feel all alone at times. King David did, as he says in Psalms 10:1:

Why standest thou afar off, oh Lord? Why hidest thou thy in times of trouble?

Sometimes you have to seek out others and let them know that you need them. And sometimes, you'll find out who your true friends are—who'll be there for you and who won't. It's important never to assume that people know what you need from them. Let people know if you're feeling hurt or alone. Tell them you need them. You deserve love and support, and sometimes you need to check in with those around you and remind them of just that.

Never Trust a Flatterer

I'M SO SORRY TO BE the one to tell you this, but you know how when you go to a department store and the salesperson tells you how thin you look in those pants, or the guy behind the counter gives that special smile to you alone? Well, yeah, they're paid to do it. And as long as they think that there's a chance that you might swipe some plastic and head home with a shopping bag full of their products, they're going to keep telling you exactly what they think that you want to hear. In Psalm 12, King David takes on phonies and flatterers:

> They speak falsehood every one with
> his neighbor; with flattering lip, and
> with a double heart, do they speak.

He then goes on to suggest that God deal pretty harshly with these insincere folks:

> May the Lord cut off all flattering lips,
> the tongue that speaketh proud things!

For the rest of us, though, it's probably just a better idea to cut off contact with people who just can't seem to be straight about anything. Honesty might not always be the best policy, but it sure beats never knowing when someone is being sincere or just saying what they think you want to hear.

On Feeling Vulnerable

IT'S AMAZING TO THINK that one of the greatest kings in biblical history—one known thousands of years after his death for his legendary adventures and gift of poetry—could be so vulnerable and insecure at times. In Psalm 13, King David pours out his heart to his God:

> *How long, Lord? Will you forget me*
> *forever? How long will you hide your*
> *face from me? How long must I wrestle*
> *with my thoughts and day after day*
> *have sorrow in my heart?*

We've all had moments (days, weeks, months, years) of deep desolation when it feels as though we've been abandoned by those we most rely on. In this Psalm, David bares his soul and explains that he feels all alone and, worse, he fears that his enemy will rejoice in his own suffering. Who hasn't felt this way? One of the hardest things possible is to tell those we love and rely on that we need them. Vulnerability isn't a character flaw or sign of weakness; it's simply another facet of being a caring, loving human being.

What's Ancient Can Be New Again

WE'VE ESTABLISHED THAT there's nothing new under the sun—only new ways to talk or do or cook or sing about it. There's a lot of personal angst in Psalm 17, and I'm struck by in this short verse:

Keep me as the apple of the eye,
hide me in the shadow of thy wings.

I'll be honest, I never had any idea of where the origin of the expression "the apple of my eye" came from. I always thought it was just some quaint saying that originated in America and became an idiom. As for the second part, it's lovely and so evocative. Sort of like the Bette Midler song that was so popular some years back "The Wind Beneath My Wings."

Sometimes if you feel less than inspired by the ancient texts, it might be fun to reread them and try to figure out what inspired modern thought or culture.

What Do You Believe In?

I GREW UP IN A HOUSEHOLD that valued knowledge and a thirst for learning. And while I was raised as an observant Jew, I was also raised with an extended worldview. At our Friday night Shabbat table, we would discuss politics and culture and books and everything and nothing at all. We chanted the proper blessings over wine and challah and we sang the traditional Hebrew melodies, but we also sang American folk songs and slave spirituals. Because my parents were both Holocaust survivors and had each endured and survived so much, my father—who was a slave laborer to the Nazis at the age of 11—felt it important that we share not only the Jewish experience and the American experience, but the slave experience as well.

My family was different from most of my friends'. I went to a private, religious all-girls school where everyone had a somewhat similar background to my own and a mostly homologous and very rigid belief system. However, as I made my way into the world, I encountered people of different faiths and with different outlooks. I was exposed to people who believed in Jesus or Allah or Buddha or Gaia. And while I was initially troubled to imagine that someone could believe so differently than I,

I realized ultimately that for people of great faith, it's the faith that matters most. And I imagine that's what drew you to this book, no matter what your religious practice—even if you have none at all.

In Psalm 14, King David struggles to find people who do good. And he says:

> *The fool hath said in his heart:*
> *"There is no God"; they have dealt*
> *corruptly, they have done abominably; there*
> *is none that doeth good.*

Though I can't presume to know what the people David mentions were actually like, I know that my own thinking has changed radically over the years. I think believing in something is what matters most. Believe in nature or believe in love or believe that by doing the right thing you can make some difference to another human being or an entire generation. There are those who say that God is in the details, and others who say that God is in every blade of grass. I say that God is where you find him or her. And for me at least, God is in hope.

Ancient vs. Modern Idolatry

ALONG WITH THE BEAUTIFUL poetry and effusive words of devotion, there's an awful lot of vengeful, bloody, or violent imagery present in the Book of Psalms. In Chapter 16, David says:

> *Let the idols of them be multiplied*
> *that make suit unto another; their drink-*
> *offerings of blood will I not offer, nor*
> *take their names upon my lips.*

There's been a lot of dispute about the notion of what those blood offerings actually entailed. In ancient times, animal sacrifice was quite common, and it's been said that those practicing the darker arts would actually drink the blood or mix it with their wine. Pretty gross and archaic, right?

Then again, this chapter has elements that feel incredibly timely. It feels like our own modern celebrity culture creates new idols by the minute, famous for a season and, for the most part, famous only for being famous. If you look at popular books, film, and television, it seems that blood-drinking underworld types become more popular by the nanosecond.

Perhaps one takeaway from this particular chapter could be the notion that, sometimes it's best just to resist the all-pervasive push to read about and know about what's trending at the moment. With every update readily available at your fingertips and across a multitude of screens, sometimes the best thing that you can do is shut off the outside world and think about what actually interests you or makes you happy.

Who's Your Rock?

CLICHÉS BECOME CLICHÉS for a reason: The strength or impact of the sayings or expressions are so right and appropriate, they have the same impact for thousands of years. In Psalm 18, King David says:

> *The Lord is my rock, and my fortress,*
> *and my deliverer. My God, my rock,*
> *in him I take refuge; my shield, and*
> *my horn of salvation, my high tower.*

I can't claim to know what a horn of salvation is. But I do know that there are some people in your life who form the bedrock or foundations of your existence. And when other people disappear because they envy your success or can't handle your great despair, your rock or rocks are always and unconditionally there for you.

I used to joke that I don't recommend cancer. Going through that part of my life taught me lessons I never wanted to learn. But more than anything, it taught me that my mother and sister must have cores of pure granite for the way that they unflaggingly and unflinchingly stood by me through every excruciating moment. My friends Ken, Erik, Heidi, and Chelsea were also like unwavering lights that

guided me through that darkest tunnel and worst time of my life.

And here's a lesson that I never expected to learn and I think you should consider: You can never predict just who will prove to be your rock. And sometimes they'll be that rock for you just when you need them and then melt away back into the sidelines again.

Who's your rock?

The Glory of Nature

PSALM 19 IS PACKED with luscious imagery and metaphors in which God reveals himself through nature. I love the way it begins: "The heavens declare the glory of God, and the firmament showeth his handiwork."

I used the most accepted English translations of the Psalms for the majority of quotes and excerpts used in this book. In rereading the Hebrew version though, I noted that the heavens are described using the word *misaprim*, as in "tells stories," and the earth was also described with another word, *magid*, which literally means "telling." So in the version that I prefer:

> *The heavens tell stories about the glory of God and the earth tells of His handiwork.*

I love to lose myself in long walks where I try to take in the beauty peeking through the long concrete blocks near where I live. I used to imagine God as an artist, painting the world in the most breathtaking ways. This Psalm, though, made me think of the heavens and earth taking a more active role and using their individual elements to tell their own stories.

Psalm 19 is fairly universally recognized and beloved among a collection rich with beauty and wisdom. It's included in the Jewish Sabbath services, and C.S. Lewis said, "I take this to be the greatest poem in the Psalter and one of the greatest lyrics in the world."

There's a lot of lovely imagery, including a strong use of nature in Psalm 19. I ponder over this one quite a bit and believe that the metaphor of the reach of god is as all-encompassing as the sun's brightness, which in turn is compared to: "The joy of a bridegroom coming out of his chamber" as well as "rejoiceth as a strong man to run his course." And there's also:

> *More to be desired are they than gold,*
> *yea, than much fine gold; sweeter also*
> *than honey and the honeycomb.*

Whatever you find to be true about this Psalm, the images speak of beauty and strength and sweetness and an overall glow in the power of strong belief.

Short but Potent

PSALM 19 ENDS OFF with a prayer within itself that is also used at the end of many prayers:

> *Let the words of my mouth*
> *and the meditation of my heart*
> *be acceptable before thee, oh*
> *Lord, my rock, and my redeemer.*

It's King David, in the guise of humble poet, saying that he hopes his words have found favor. It's almost like hanging up the phone with someone dear to you. You might have been talking for hours about things mundane or meaningful, but suddenly when it comes time to say good-bye, you get a little bit mushy and want those last few words to really count. When was the last time that you told someone you love the reasons that you love them?

In Between Days

THERE'S SO MUCH HIDDEN WISDOM in the ancient texts that it's sometimes easy to lose oneself in trying to understand them. It's been said that the 70 words in Psalm 20 represent the 70-year exile between the destruction of the first temple and the building of the second. Some people find it comforting to recite this Psalm when a woman is in labor, which presents a different kind of exile for both the unborn child and its mother: the state of not knowing yet, waiting, anticipating, and full of pain while waiting for the next stage—the difference being that if all goes well, there's a lifetime of love ahead.

In the middle of the Psalm there's a short line that seems to pair faith with courage: *They bend and fall, but we rise and stand firm.*

It can feel crazy-making to feel stuck between the past and the present, but it's crucial to remember not to be so focused on the next stage that you all but forget to revel in the here and now.

Find Your Strength

I GUESS THIS IS THE POINT for some further confessions. Not only did I attend private, religious all-girls school, I also attended religious all-girls camp. Yeah, that was fun. That said, before I was old enough to realize that I might be missing out on boys and other adventures I couldn't quite comprehend, I really did love the girl-power camaraderie of summer camp. And part of that involved singing lots of Hebrew songs at the tops of our very young lungs.

The last few verses of Psalm 20 are part of one such popular song. Though I was still too young to understand the words fully, I felt the intention behind them, and it was powerful:

Some trust in chariots, and some in horses;
but we will make mention of the name of
the Lord our God. They are bowed down
and fallen; but we are risen, and stand upright.

From this vantage point in my life, I take that rousing verse to tell us not to be distracted by the trappings of power, or of the new and shiny or overtly impressive. Trust in your own belief system. Believe in what you know is right. You're strong enough to know what's authentic.

Count Your Blessings

Do you ever have days when you're just feeling incredibly and impossibly fortunate in your life? Along with running from his enemies and feeling the heartache of having been betrayed by those closest to him, King David had moments where he just felt inspired to sing about his great good fortune.

In Psalm 21, David speaks in the third person when describing himself and God's generosity to him:

> *Thou hast given him his heart's desire, and the*
> *request of his lips thou hast not withholden…*
> *For thou meetest him with choicest blessings;*
> *Thou settest a crown of fine gold on his head.*

David didn't take his position for granted, but rather made a point of listing the different gifts he'd been given.

It can feel corny to be reminded to count your blessings, but sometimes it really is the only thing to lift you out of a funk. My brother frequently jokes that he's more fortunate than most kings, since he has a bounty of gourmet foods that weren't even available to the wealthiest men or monarchs in ancient times. Sometimes having a better day can be dependent on something as small as realizing just how lucky you already are.

Live Life

THERE'S A SHORT VERSE, or mini-sentence in Psalm 21:5 that struck a chord for me. David is still speaking in the third person when he says:

He asked life of Thee, Thou gavest it him.

For a very long time, I did not talk publicly about having faced a life-threatening illness. I figured that I gave enough of my life to cancer; I had no intention of giving it even a single minute more. But as others told me about their own battles or family members facing the *Big Bad*, I realized that I could help them and inspire them or cheer them on. So, I mention it in this book, because cancer changed me in many ways. But cancer isn't who I am, and it certainly doesn't define me. It's just one thing that happened to me on my very colorful journey.

Let's face it, when things are going okay, most of us take not only the good things in our life for granted—we pretty much take life for granted. And when I was at my worst and trapped in bed and staring out my window like some forgotten heroine in a never printed O. Henry story, I wanted nothing more than life. I wanted the ordinary again. I wanted to meet my friends for lunch or complain about the crowded subways. I wanted to eat without feeling nauseated.

I wanted to shower again without fear of falling. I just wanted my life back. Not the daydream fantasy version I kept waiting for, but the ordinary day-to-day life I'd crafted for myself for better or worse.

There's a modern Israeli expression that I've always loved. Whereas Americans might tell someone heading out on a trip to "have fun," Israelis say *Ta'Asee Chayim*, which literally translated means, "Make life."

As someone who's faced pretty much the worst that life has to offer, I say to you: Make life. Live life. Don't count down the days until your next raise or vacation, or ignore the moment of pure joy that you might find unexpectedly. It's your life—live it!

On Feeling Abandoned

IN PSALM 22, it feels like King David is having a dark night of the soul. He talks about how abandoned he feels:

> *My God, my God, why hast Thou forsaken me, and art far from my help at the words of my cry?*

The Psalm goes on in that vein for a while. In the original Hebrew, David uses the word Eli for "my god." It isn't one of the more formal names for God, who is said to have dozens or hundreds of names. And unlike some of the other names of God, *El* or *Eli*, (my God) can be seen as an expression signifying closeness, which then magnifies his feeling of abandonment. And every time something is repeated, much less the name of God, the sages say it is for a specific purpose. The shock here is doubled. We were so close, how could you leave me?

The words of *Eli*, *Eli*, from this Psalm are used in prayers in many other places, including the Rosh Hashanah, or Jewish New Year, prayers. It's an incredibly mournful prayer, and the recurring theme is between David and those seeking blessings for the year ahead and respite from the bad things in the year that was. And worse, it suggests

the shared notion of feeling so close to someone who has left them feeling abandoned.

I've never subscribed to the notion of there being one way to believe, one way to connect, or one way to pray. And at some times in our lives, we all feel abandoned or unsure of our own beliefs. Some feel most comfortable using their own words at their own times (I'm one of those people). But sometimes seeing the words used to express that gnawing abandonment felt by King David can offer comfort and a sense of camaraderie in particularly bleak times. Even King David felt alone and bereft at times. You're not alone in feeling alone.

Rediscovering the Familiar

PSALM 23, "The Lord is my Shepherd," is probably one of the more well-known and universally popular prayers. It crosses not only religious boundaries, being popular with both Jews and Christian religions alike, but is also prominently featured in film and song.

There's a reason for its popularity. Besides the beautifully composed words and imagery, the turns of phrase work as well together as they do on their own:

> *The Lord is my shepherd; I shall not want.*
>
> *He maketh me to lie down in green pastures;*
> *He leadeth me beside the still waters.*
>
> *He restoreth my soul; He guideth me in*
> *straight paths for His name's sake.*
>
> *Yea, though I walk through the valley*
> *of the shadow of death, I will fear no evil,*
> *for Thou art with me;*
>
> *Thy rod and thy staff, they comfort me.*
>
> *Thou preparest a table before me in the*
> *presence of mine enemies;*
>
> *Thou hast anointed my head with oil;*
> *my cup runneth over.*

Surely goodness and mercy shall follow me
all the days of my life;

and I shall dwell in the house of
the Lord forever.

In reading and re-reading this Psalm over the years, I've come to realize one thing to be true: with every reading, something new strikes me or speaks to me. Despite the fact that I have such a comfortable working knowledge of these verses, each time I read them I discover something, or different words feel applicable to my life stage or circumstances.

On reading this today, these words struck me: "He restoreth my soul." What a wonderful concept. So many people that I know talk about feeling burnt out or needing to reinvent themselves. I love the idea that it's possible to restore your soul in some way or form. And this Psalm reminds me not to always look at things the exact same way, but to find a brand-new way of seeing even the same old things.

Daily Indignities

THERE ARE MANY BLESSINGS for morning that are supposed to set the path for the day ahead. One in particular, *Ha'Mavir Shaina* or "Who Removes Sleep," doesn't just thank God for allowing us to awake, but follows with about 15 requests for the rest of the day. Two in particular struck me, but the wording is a bit difficult to explain in English, so I'll paraphrase. The prayer asks that we not be put into the path of temptation, and that we not be placed into a humiliating situation. If you've ever suffered through a morning commute where you're closely packed against total strangers, you know the endless opportunities for rage and humiliation—and that's only the beginning of the day. Like praying for a parking spot or sending up a wish that the rain hold off until you're in your car, some prayers seem composed to ward off a challenging day.

Moving Forward or Standing Still?

ABRAHAM ISAAC KOOK (Rabbi or "Rav Kook"), was a renowned Torah scholar of the early 20th century. He had an interesting insight into Psalm 24:

Who shall ascend into the mountain of the Lord? and who shall stand in his holy place?

I won't go into the deeper meanings of his words (mainly because a lot of them are so deep as to feel confusing), but one notion that really struck me is that ascending or standing still requires use of your legs—whether your legs are holding you steadfast or frozen by fear of change to where you've always been; whether your legs are straining to move you forward or elevating you to rise to another level. This one body part is able to keep you where you always were or allow you to become transformed.

While Rav Kook's insights had to do with the elevation of the spiritual self, I like the idea of using this as a metaphor to challenge your own status quo constantly. Sometimes things really are best exactly as they are. Other times, you need to propel yourself forward and climb over every stumbling block that keeps you from becoming the next and better version of yourself.

Don't Live in the Past

IN PSALM 25, DAVID IMPLORES his God not to judge him by what he once was:

Remember not the sins of my youth,
nor my transgressions; according to
thy mercy remember thou me, for
thy goodness' sake, oh Lord.

I know just how he felt.

I'm sure that after reading about some of my background you think I have always been the quintessential good girl and pious soul. And I was in many ways. But I also always questioned what I was taught and rebelled against my stringent religious upbringing. And I was a bit of a wild child and party girl in my teens and early twenties. Okay, throughout my twenties and some of my early thirties. But the thing is, I've moved on. I've gotten a lot out of my system and have mellowed and found a version of myself that I'm comfortable with most of the time. I've always loved this line in the Crosby, Stills and Nash song "Suite: Judy Blue Eyes": "Don't let the past remind us of what we are not now." Yet sometimes when I run into people from my distant past or when they connect with me on social media, they remember a very

different person from the one that I am now. And I don't want to be that version of myself anymore. That's my past.

It's hard to grow and evolve. Harder still to try to remain crammed into a version of yourself that no longer fits. It hurts to let go sometimes. It hurts even more to live your life for others. Stop living in your past and focus on your future.

Thanksgiving

I LOVE THANKSGIVING and look forward to it all year. It gives me a chance to think about all of the incredible things in my life for which I'm grateful. And sometimes, as I make my way down the list, I realize that the great things really outweigh the crummy ones. In Psalm 26 David lists the things that set him apart from the less righteous or worthy; one of them is:

> *To proclaim thanksgiving with a loud voice*
> *and to recite all Your wonders.*

Being grateful for what you have really is an incredible quality. Some people seem to take everything for granted, and when things don't go their way, they complain about every minute detail. But focusing on the good gives you less time to obsess about and magnify the less thrilling aspects of your life.

Don't Always Push
for a Resolution

WE ALL HAVE DIFFERENT STYLES of relating. Some people are easygoing and nothing seems to drag them down; others tend to nitpick and find the worst in even the best efforts. And we all have different styles of arguing and making up as well. King David says:

> *Hear the voice of my supplications,*
> *when I cry unto Thee.*

It makes sense. He is a human being calling out urgently to God with his deep need to be heard and then helped. But with some people, it can work differently. Sometimes the worst thing that you can do is to try to force someone to listen to you when they're just not ready. Sometimes if you've hurt someone or betrayed someone or acted in an insensitive manner, you just have to wait until they're ready to listen to your apology.

There Is Great Strength in Calm

ONE OF MY FAVORITE PEOPLE on earth is also probably the calmest person that I know. He isn't calm because he lives a life of leisure. He's actually an emergency doctor—definitely not the most relaxing profession on earth. As someone who has been accused of being somewhat dramatic (I know, I was shocked too!), I value someone who's strong enough to remain calm in nearly any situation. And I love this line in Psalm 29:

The Lord shall grant strength to His people;
the Lord shall bless His people with peace.

For me it brings to mind Lewis, and the way that he brings peace and lends strength to those around him. Sometimes our greatest strengths aren't necessarily in showing our power, but in being secure enough to share our more gentle side.

Things Will Be Better
in the Morning

WHAT IS IT ABOUT the wee hours of the night that make problems seem worse? F. Scott Fitzgerald summed it up perfectly when he wrote that, "In a real dark night of the soul it is always three o'clock in the morning." It's hard to be reasonable when all you can do is lie awake and panic. In Psalm 30, King David says:

> For His anger is but for a moment,
> His favor is for a lifetime;
> weeping may tarry for the night,
> but joy cometh in the morning.

There are two wonderful bits of wisdom there. It's impossible not to get angry sometimes, but it's important to let that anger go and let go of those bad feelings. Even if it feels like life is out to get you sometimes, and you spend the night weeping your heart out, things will almost always feel better in the morning.

Don't Let Your Problems Define You

PEOPLE TEND TO HAVE NICKNAMES based on the way that they look or the things that they love, but why on earth would you want the worst parts of your life to define you? In Psalm 31, King David says:

For my life is spent in sorrow, and
my years in sighing; my strength faileth
because of mine iniquity, and
my bones are wasted away.

So many people obsess about their looks and worry about looking old. They despair that their laugh lines give away their age, but all that their laugh lines really say about them is that so far they've had a life filled with laughter and that they've spent their years well. Why spend time sitting around being miserable when you can use that time to enjoy life and friendships, and take joy in every moment?

Be True to Your Heart

THERE'S A JEWISH CONCEPT called *Gematria*, which can assign numerical value to key words or phrases and can almost seem like numerical anagrams. When I looked at Psalm 32, I immediately was struck by the word that the numbers spelled out. In the Hebrew alphabet, 32 is *Lamed Bet* and the word spelled by those initials is Lev or "heart." There's also a notion that certain Psalms have special significance, or can be said to ask for help with specific needs. There are Psalms said when someone is ill, or when someone needs courage, and this Psalm can be said when seeking true love or a soul mate. The Psalm ends:

> *Shout for joy, all ye*
> *that are upright in heart.*

There's a special kind of joy in finding the person that makes your heart sing and in knowing that you've trusted your heart and recognized someone worth loving.

Find a Peacemaker

THERE'S A YIDDISH EXPRESSION that won't come across quite as juicy in English; loosely translated it means "Don't tease a bully." In other words, why look for trouble or start up with someone who's sure to give you more than you bargained for? In Psalm 43:1 King David asks God to:

Plead my cause.

The exact wording is *Rivah Rivee*, which literally translated means fight my fight or argue my argument. Sometimes you're just too close to a situation to see it clearly anymore. Or sometimes you're just too weary or beaten down by circumstances that are out of your control. In those instances, you'd probably overreact and escalate a more manageable situation. Try to have a calm friend or someone in a position of authority plead your case. And if you see someone dear to you going through a similar problem, try to do the same for them.

Might Doesn't Necessarily Make Right

WHEN I THINK ABOUT the strongest people that I know, physical prowess generally has precious little to do with it. My friend Heidi doesn't always have an easy time of things; she's mother to a special-needs teen and faces daily challenges relating to his care. But Heidi never falters, and she certainly never gives up on him. And when life throws even more challenges her way, she and her husband, Mo, face them together with grace and humor and an iron will. And they form an invincible army of two. In Psalm 33 King David says:

> *The king is not saved with a vast army;*
> *A mighty man will not be rescued*
> *by great strength.*

Sometimes the greatest strength comes from within. And learning to face life head on without being crushed by the obstacles in your way can make you stronger than Superman.

Deceitful Friends

I'VE NEVER QUITE TAKEN to the notion of "frenemies" or friends who are actually enemies. Why would anyone willingly surround themselves with those who secretly wish them harm? Psalm 35 is packed with all of the evil things that so-called friends can do, and it's a pretty harsh litany. At one point, though, King David says:

Let them be ashamed and abashed together that rejoice at my hurt; let them be clothed with shame and confusion that magnify themselves against me.

It's almost a poignant expression of rage. There's enough sadness and natural disasters in this world without having to worry that those who are supposed to be closest to you might actually wish you harm. Cut them loose. And give yourself permission not to accept every friend request on social media either. Some friendships are better left in the past for a reason.

A Note on Rashi:
Ask the Right Questions

ONE OF THE MOST PROLIFIC commenters on the Talmud was the medieval French scholar Rabbi Shlomo Yitzchaki, better known as Rashi. As a young girl I learned to read Rashi's commentary in the original Aramaic; more than that, I learned to always look for Rashi's questions. Rashi had a unique way of offering commentary; instead of simply offering his insights, he offered a solution and readers were meant to look for the question being answered. Questions could be tricky or matter of fact, based on word usage or tenses used. Learning to always wonder about Rashi's questions, means always looking for a deeper meaning in words or quotes or prayer. In reading some of the Psalms and some of Rashi's commentary, I invite you to try to figure out for yourself what his questions might have been, starting with Psalm 36.

Don't Let Negative People Get a Foot in the Door

IN READING PSALM 36:12, I was struck by the use of the words:

Let not the foot of pride overtake me.

Rashi's commentary on this verse says not to let even the foot of an evil person be with you when you're rewarded for doing the right thing. This raises the question, why use the word "foot"? I take it to mean not to let the wrong people get even a toehold in your life. Sometimes it feels easier to let someone push their way into your life, even when you know they're bad for you. In this context, it's the metaphors that are strongest. Take a minute to think about the people in your world, even in your social networks. Do they enhance your sense of well-being, or do they fill you with regret? Does seeing an email or text from them fill you with joy or a sense of dread?

Don't Overthink Everything

THESE WORDS ARE USED three separate times in Psalm 37:

Fret not thyself.

When a particular word or phrase is repeated, there's usually a very good reason for it. In this particular instance, readers are urged not to harm themselves by worrying about evildoers, not to spend time worrying about those who are better off than they are, and not to simply fret for the sake of fretting.

A wise woman once advised me, "Don't let what you don't have ruin what you do have." I'll take it one step further: Don't let what everyone else might have ruin what you already have. Instead, focus on the good things in your life instead of working yourself into a state about what you think you should have or should have achieved.

Prayers as Poetry

THERE ARE DAYS when I don't feel a strong connection to the ancient prayers at all. Sure, the
words are wonderful, but they don't always touch
my heart in quite the same way. On those days,
I prefer to think of the texts as beautiful poetry.
At the end of the Sabbath there are some songs
sung and prayers chanted that include blessings
and hopes for the week ahead. There's always a
tinge of sadness on leaving the Sabbath behind and
much in the way that most people get the Sunday
night blues, there can be a similar sense of Saturday
evening melancholia. These short, simple blessings
are so full of promise and bring hope for a better
week ahead:

And may God give to you the dew
of the heavens and the richest of the
lands, and abundant grain and wine.

Words Like Arrows

ONE OF THE BEST ASPECTS of our very interactive world is the nearly universal ability to interact with strangers, politicians, and celebrities through a few keyboard strokes. But as we become more available and accessible, we also become more potentially cruel or vulnerable. While Johann Sebastian Bach chose Psalm 38:4 as the opening chorus for one of his cantatas, I was more struck by the verse right before it:

> For thine arrows are gone deep into me.

In the past few years, there have been many campaigns discussing the dangers of bullying, but sometimes it's a more subtle type of slight that cuts most deeply: snide comments about a boss or coworker, anonymous comments left online, or thinly veiled sarcasm that isn't very funny. Face to face or online, choose your words carefully, because they can't always be retracted, and sometimes they live on long after you regret uttering them.

Ancient Prayer in Modern Culture

ONE OF THE LOVELIER CUSTOMS in ancient prayer is *Birkat Kohanim*, which translates to the "Blessing of the Priests." The first and second temples were destroyed thousands of years ago and there aren't actually priests in the Jewish faith. On special occasions, though, those of priestly heritage bless the congregation. It's a bit otherworldly to see descendants of the ancient families, covered in their white prayer shawls (you're not supposed to peek during the prayers) reciting:

> *May the Lord make His face shed light*
> *upon you and be gracious unto you—*
> *May the Lord lift up His face unto you*
> *and give you peace.*

It's a prayer also recited before bed and during numerous times throughout the liturgy, yet it gains special significance here. It's also worth noting that Leonard Nimoy, who played Mr. Spock on *Star Trek*, was raised in an observant Jewish household. Nimoy borrowed the accompanying hand gestures as the Vulcan hand salute that meant, "Live long and prosper."

Be Ageless

WHENEVER I'M FEELING BUMMED by a particular birthday or calendar date, I think about that Satchel Paige quote: "How old would you be if you didn't know how old you are?" When going through chemo a few years back, I'd probably have told you I was about 92 years old. I could barely get out of bed most days and my most memorable accomplishment was retrieving the mail on my own. These days though, I feel younger and more optimistic than ever. I've lived through the worst and am ready to reclaim my best. In Psalm 39:6, King David says:

> *Behold, thou hast made my days as*
> *hand-breadths; and mine age is*
> *as nothing before thee.*

Sure, some days are better than others, and some birthdays feel momentous, but in the grand scheme of things, you're so much more than the number on your driver's license.

Be Strong and Courageous

SOME PEOPLE FACE IMMINENT danger on a daily basis. Those with military careers, law enforcement officials, and firefighters quite literally walk through fire to keep others safe. But that doesn't minimize the crushing stresses of a more typical life. Daily life can be fraught with incredibly challenging and frightening situations. It's been said that most people fear public speaking even more than death. Add to that the myriad tiny indignities we face, and some days all you want to do is crawl back under the covers and hide from life. King David had his share of bad days, and in Psalm 27 he uses an expression frequently repeated in Joshua:

Be strong and courageous.

When life feels harder than it should, those simple words might just help you get through.

Your Theme Song

IN THE BEGINNING OF PSALM 40, King David talks about needing salvation, about being rescued from a slimy pit and set on solid ground—wonderful imagery to be sure. A bit later, in Verse 4, he says:

And He hath put a new song in my mouth.

This really put a smile on my face. I've always thought that, much like movies or superheroes, people should have their own theme songs: songs to cheer us on or lift our spirits, songs to tell us that better days are ahead or remind us of times when we were incredibly happy. In this Psalm, David articulates the fact that sometimes we need to reset the tune in our head or heart to reflect our changed circumstances or outlook.

Don't Eat Your Heart Out

HAVE YOU EVER FOUND YOURSELF using a favorite expression or idiom and then wondering about its origin? In reading through all of these ancient texts, I began noticing certain seemingly quaint turns of phrase that are likely predecessors for common modern expressions. In Psalm 42:4 King David says:

My tears have been my food day and night.

It's an expression that I thought was unfamiliar to me until I read the commentary by Rashi. He says that we can surmise from this wording that anguish can actually satisfy a person. And I think we've all met people like that—people so deeply enmeshed in their own bad moods that their sadness actually nourishes them. While we all need to wallow in self-pity every now and again, here's hoping that we can pull ourselves back out before it becomes habit-forming.

Unconditional Love

IN *PEREK SHIRA*, THE SONG OF CREATION, there are two separate chapters dedicated to the prayer of the dog. The first, Chapter 5:17, deals with the prayer of the hound (some say this is a greyhound or more outdoorsy kind of dog). The second, Chapter 7:8 (originally found in Psalms 95:6), is actually the final prayer in *Perek Shira* and deals with complete and utter acceptance and adoration as shown by a pet dog to its beloved master.

> *The dog says: "Come, let us prostrate ourselves and bow, let us kneel before God our Maker."*

It's almost sweet to imagine what the most loyal of pets, a dog, might say if given the chance: No expectations. No demands for reciprocal emotion. No temper tantrums or pouting. Only simple acceptance and adoration. If you've ever had your heart broken, it can be hard to learn to love again, much less learn to love with a full heart. But there's a special joy in allowing oneself simply to adore the object of one's affections.

Darkest Before Dawn

THE *SELICHOT* (PLURAL FOR *Selichah*, the Hebrew word for forgiveness) are incredibly somber prayers said on the days leading into the High Holy Days on the Jewish calendar. The *Selichot* contain the words *b'ashmoret haboker*, which can be translated to dawn, or:

The beginning of the morning

Adding to the mystical, almost spooky mood, *Selichot* are generally recited after midnight and before dawn. Unlike the way it is celebrated in other cultures, the Jewish New Year is fraught with prayer and fervent hopes for forgiveness and a better year ahead. In my mind, at least, the *Selichot* symbolize a time when things feel darkest, but if you can get through the hurdles ahead, you can start the new day or new year over even better than before.

Slow to Anger

THERE'S AN INTERESTING PRAYER, or list, called the *Shalosh Esrei Middot* that is contained within the *Selichot* prayers and is recited on Yom Kippur and many Jewish holidays. These words originate in Exodus 34:6–7 and are said to be the 13 Attributes of God as told to Moses. What's most interesting about this prayer is the list of earthly attributes attributed to the almighty, qualities that we as people are encouraged to emulate. Included are *Erech Appayim* (slow to anger); *Emet* (truth), and *Noseh avon, Noseh peshah,* and *Noseh chatah* (forgiving of three individual separate types of wrongdoing, transgressions, and sins). Forgiving your enemies or those who have wronged you isn't one of the recommended or necessary ancient biblical philosophies. Trying to contain or overcome your anger even when you're well aware of the transgressions of those closest to you, certainly is.

The Qualities of Forgiveness

MUCH HAS BEEN WRITTEN about the quality of mercy, but not a lot about the quality of forgiveness. In researching the High Holy Days prayers, I came across writings and commentary by a sixteenth-century Kabbalist, Rabbi Moshe Cordovero, known as the "Ramak." In his book *Tomer Devorah*, which means the "Palm Tree of Deborah," the Ramak discusses three main qualities of forgiveness: *Selichah*, which means forgiveness; *Mechilah*, a word that means the equivalent of wiping [the slate] clean; and *Kapparah*, which best translates to "atonement." In Jewish tradition, if you've wronged someone, you're expected to ask their forgiveness three separate times and on three separate occasions. If they still refuse after you've asked sincerely, you're considered forgiven. We all have different fighting styles and we certainly all have different methods of forgiveness. Sometimes it hurts more to hold onto old grievances than to let them and the person who wronged you be relegated to your past.

Kol Nidrei: All Vows

Yom Kippur, the Day of Atonement, is the most important day of the Jewish calendar. *Kol Nidrei* or All Vows services are the most well-known. Despite being one of the most famous prayers of Jewish liturgy, *Kol Nidrei*'s centuries-old wording is simple and composed of a statement in which vows, future or past, are nullified, followed by a standard list of Aramaic terms for vows. Some promises were made to be broken. Some believe that *Kol Nidrei* was popularized by Jews forced to convert to Christianity during the Spanish Inquisition. In this way, they could make it clear at least once a year that they'd converted under pains of death, but still retained their true faith. Faith can be a tricky issue, as can making or keeping promises. One imagines that on a personal or universal level, it's important to stay true to yourself and your beliefs.

Don't Be a Gossip

WE LIVE IN A CULTURE OBSESSED with gossip. And while it can feel like a victimless crime to rehash the latest dirt about celebrities or politicians, it can have a trickle-down effect and lead to talking smack about your own inner circle. Alice Roosevelt was known for having a pillow embroidered with the quote: "If you can't say something good about someone, sit right here by me." But what happens when you turn your back on someone like that? A few years back, a series of studies indicated that people don't think poorly about the person being gossiped about, but rather the person doing the gossiping. In Psalm 34, King David says:

> *Keep thy tongue from evil, and*
> *thy lips from speaking deceitfully.*

It seems like a pretty sound policy. Don't speak unkindly about people, and try not to spread untrue rumors, because you really wouldn't like it if everyone were talking about you.

You Will Be Fine

IN JEWISH MYSTICISM and Kabbalah, the number seven has many significant attributes. The world was created in seven days; certain phrases are repeated seven times during High Holy Day prayers. And some believe repeating prayers seven times means they reach through the seven layers [heavens] separating God from people.

On one of the worst days of my life, the day I was diagnosed with cancer, Doctor Mark Persky tried to assure me that despite the grim prognosis, I would in fact be fine. He urged me to look at him, and I refused. Dr. Persky walked over and stood right next to me and said directly into my ear, "You will be fine." And I still refused to look at him. He repeated it. And then he repeated it again. I sat still and frozen as he continued to repeat himself over and over, and I realized that I'd been unintentionally counting. Whether Dr. Persky realized it or not, he'd repeated, "You will be fine" a total of seven times. Finally, I nodded. Curtly. Angrily. But I could not escape his words. And he was right. I am fine. But the thing is, that sometimes we need to be reminded over and over of something until we know it to be true. And believe me when I tell you this: though things might seem awful at times, you will be fine too.

Our Father, Our King

*A*VINU *M*ALKEINU IS ONE of the more moving prayers recited on both Rosh Hashanah and Yom Kippur. For some, it's also said during the 10 days between the two holidays, known as the 10 Days of Repentance. It says, we understand that we may not be worthy, yet we are asking for help anyway. Beautiful words are paired with a haunting melody frequently sung in something of a call and response between the prayer leader and the congregation. And it is an awe-inspiring thing to be in a room full of people singing their hearts out. One of the more famous verses almost always sung aloud is:

> *Our father, our King, graciously answer us, although we are without merits; deal with us charitably and lovingly save us.*

If you want to blow your mind a little, track down the industrial-sounding instrumental recording "Our Father, Our King," by Scottish post-rock band Mogwai.

But How Are You Blessed?

IT'S BECOME SOMETHING of a cliché to hear people say they are blessed. But when it comes right down to it, there are many miniscule details that go into day-to-day life for which we should be grateful. Silly things like finding a parking spot, or drinking the perfect cup of coffee, make a gray morning less oppressive. Huge things like a loving partner or healthy children or a fulfilling job or cozy home—they aren't small things, and they shouldn't be taken for granted. The traditional blessings can be broken down into several categories: blessings on pleasurable experiences, blessings when performing a commandment, and blessings of praise. So the next time you're ready to consider yourself blessed, take an extra few seconds to realize the level of detail that makes this moment worth noting.

Body and Soul

SOMETIMES WHAT AILS YOU is physical. Sometimes—on the other hand—pain comes deep
from within an emotional place and can feel as
dark and overwhelming as a major illness. In Psalm
41, King David talks not just about his enemies,
but also about his history of physical and emotional ailments. And when he's not quite sure whom he
can trust and his enemies seem to be waiting for
him to fail, he counts on his God. In Verse 5, when
David prays for a cure for his physical ailments, he
also requests:

Be gracious unto me; heal my soul.

It's common for people to pray for someone who's
sick or ask for healing thoughts and best wishes.
This verse makes us realize that it's also okay to
ask for help when your soul hurts and you're in
emotional pain as well.

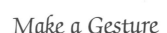

Make a Gesture

ONE OF THE MORE CURIOUS parts of ancient liturgy is the *Tashlich* or *Casting Off* ceremony. In a nutshell, on the first day of the Jewish New Year, one goes near an open source of water, says a short prayer and symbolically casts off the past year's bad deeds in the form of small pieces of bread for the fish and sea creatures. And before you start wondering what the fish did to deserve everyone's worst actions, fish are considered immune to evil actions, so it's a win/win situation. There are several times during the year when physical actions represent emotional actions or reactions and prayers said. Instead of merely offering lip service, it's a lovely way of manifesting your prayers into action.

Live a Vibrant Life

"MAY YOU LIVE UNTIL 120," or the Yiddish variant *Biz a hindred und tzvuntzig* or Hebrew *Ad Meah Ve'esrim*, is not so much an ancient prayer, as an ancient theme turned daily blessing. The ideal life span of 120 years is first mentioned in Genesis 6:3:

> And the Lord said: "My spirit shall
> not abide in man forever, for that he
> also is flesh; therefore shall his days
> be a hundred and twenty years."

It was Moses' life that inspired the blessing. In Deuteronomy 34:7 it says, "And Moses was a hundred and twenty years old when he died." While Moses lived several lifetimes, as a prince in Egypt, then prophet and leader of a nation, it was not the length of his life that was most remarkable, but the quality of it. The line continues, "His eye was not dim, nor his natural force abated." Inspiration to make each day and each year remarkable and notable.

For the Sins We've Committed

ON THE DAY of ATONEMENT there's a prayer recited of uncertain provenance, that's repeated numerous times. Each line begins *Al Chet*, which means "For the sin" and is followed by a particular transgression. The thing is that some of the wrongs we've done or admit doing, are not necessarily things we'd have thought of. And while most of us attempt to be good and decent people (at least most of the time), this list can make one feel pretty awful. I'd like to think that this list presents us with a way of focusing on the aspects of our personalities we'd like to work on in the coming year. For instance, admitting being guilty of "causeless hatred," made me realize all the petty things I might have thought about others, and the ways I hope to be able to rise above, moving forward.

A Short Confession

AN INTERESTING ASPECT of classic High Holy Day liturgy is that it doesn't have to be complicated to be potent. *Ashamnu*, translates to:

We have transgressed.

This is one of the shorter and more powerful confessional prayers. And while it's sometimes said quietly and other times recited as part of the congregation, it's a confession made directly to God. There. It's out in the open. What follows is an almost alphabetic (the Hebrew Aleph Bet) listing of the ways in which we've transgressed. And it's a pretty robust and unflinching list. In the culture of ancient prayer and repentance, though, there are three steps to achieving forgiveness: *Vidui, Charata, Kabalah al Ha'Atid*—confession, regret, future resolution. Sometimes we beat ourselves up trying to find the perfect words to make things right with a loved one. And that can lengthen the painful process of reconciliation. Sometimes it might be best off to admit the transgression and try to move forward to forgiveness.

Remind Them

WHEN I WAS IN our synagogue on Yom Kippur, I had a transcendent moment and had to catch my breath. I closed my eyes for a minute while the entire congregation was singing one of my favorite prayers, Anu Amecha which means, "We are Your Nation/People" and almost felt my soul transported to different congregations singing the same song, a century ago, two centuries ago, and even longer. The words were so potent, but the traditional melody carried those words along with it. It's a sweet prayer, in which we kind of nudge God to remember what we mean to each other. We're not random strangers asking for health, happiness, a good life, and income:

> We are Your dear ones,
> and You are our Beloved.

It's also a nice preface to asking someone for a giant favor. Remind them of your relationship and your place in their life. And try to remind them why you're worth it.

Listen to Our Voice

A BEAUTIFUL PRAYER SAID on the Day of Atonement is *Shemah Koleinu*:

Listen to our voice.

When I was in school, I would figure out my own interpretations of the ancient texts I learned. While I almost always aced my Hebrew subject exams, my teachers questioned me about the sources and origins of the *meforshim* or commentaries I supplied on tests. I explained that I'd made them up, following my own heart and instincts in seeking explanations. I'm not sure I can begin to explain just how frowned upon that was in religious girls' schools. We were meant to rely on the explanations of others—almost exclusively men. If you look at the words *Shemah Koleinu*, it feels grammatically incorrect: listen to *our voice*. For me, at least, there should be no distinction between whose voice is heard or accepted, but rather all voices raised in prayer or learning should be heard as one and considered equal.

P.S.

THE FINAL PRAYER on the Day of Atonement is *Ne'ilah*, or the Final or Concluding Service. And it's a prayer wrought with tremendous emotion—both relief at the conclusion of a day of fasting, and prayer and apprehension that perhaps you haven't said everything you could or should have. And prayers that included the words "write," as in asking that God write you into the proverbial book of life, are now replaced with "sealed."

The wording can feel ominous, that your fate is sealed for yet another year. Yet the ancient texts and faiths believe in free will above all else and the power to change. So even if you feel that all is sealed for the next year, you can turn right around and add your own postscript and continue to hope for and work for more and better in the year ahead.

Bendigamos

ONE OF THE SUBJECTS that I haven't delved into too deeply is the origins of the two most well-known subcultures of Judaism. Ashkenazic Jews originated in Eastern Europe, France, and Germany. Sephardic Jews originate from Spain, Portugal, the Middle East, and North Africa. While the origins and faith are identical, the different Diasporas (including the expulsion of the Jews from Spain during the Spanish Inquisition) resulted in different customs, observances, and prayers. So while both adhere to liturgy that is thousands of years old, there are significant differences. For instance, while Yiddish is considered the most commonly known Ashkenazic Jewish language, including elements of German and Hebrew, Ladino, composed of Spanish and Hebrew, is the Sephardic equivalent. *Bendigamos* is a lovely after-meal prayer I first learned about when visiting Congregation Shearith Israel in New York City. The origins of the prayer are said to be thousands of years old and include roots in France, Curacao, and Jamaica.

Restoring Your Soul

I T'S AN AMAZING THING to rediscover prayers
you've known since you were old enough to
speak and to find entirely new meanings in them
at different points in your life. *Elohai Neshamah*,
continues the theme of *Modeh Ani*, as a way of
thanking God for restoring one's soul each morning. The prayer begins:

> *My God, the soul that You*
> *have given me is pure.*

The prayer continues to give thanks for the soul as
long as it is contained with me (the speaker).

Have you ever seen something so entirely beautiful
and new that it took your breath away or restored
your faith? I remember the first time that I saw
the Painted Desert in Arizona. It was sunset and
my sister and I were driving through in a baby-
blue Cadillac. It was one of those perfect moments
where my soul felt brand-new again. Life can be
full of those moments, and sometimes all it takes is
stopping to marvel at the wonder of a brand-new
day full of opportunity.

Bless That Fashion

WELL, MAYBE NOT LITERALLY, but pretty close. There is a series of morning blessings that take us through the daily routine. They all start with the same few words and then continue. One of them is *Malbish Arumim*, which translates to:

Clothe the naked

I, for one, love the idea of any sort of faith, prayer, or notion that celebrates style. There seems to be a mistaken apprehension that the ancient faiths or religions unilaterally embrace asceticism. Not so. Special clothes are bought and put aside for holidays and the Sabbath. And an appreciation of beautiful clothing or the skill that goes into creating it seems in a small way to mirror an appreciation of the beauty of the universe. So when you wake up in the morning and you're giddy to wear a new pair of shoes or boots, realize that it really might be approaching some sort of a religious experience!

I Have Just What I Need

ONE OF THE MORNING BLESSINGS is *She'Asah Li Kol Tzarki*, translated to:

> *Who has provided me my every need*

For better or worse, we live in a consumer-driven culture. So, as soon as you get the next iPhone or tablet, you're probably two behind everyone else. And trying to keep up with everyone else will probably just make you miserable.

Take a look around your home or apartment. Pretty nice, huh? Just because advertisers earn a living off of your dissatisfaction is no reason to give in to it. We all like shiny, pretty things (guilty as charged), but if the past few years have taught us anything, it's that we can survive just as well with less, or with less frequent upgrades. If nothing else, take a minute or two today to appreciate all the nice things in your life.

Grant Strength to the Weary

I AM NOT A MORNING PERSON. In fact, on the rare occasion that I make it into the city for a breakfast meeting or early start to my day, I congratulate myself for the remainder of the day. I marvel at my friends and colleagues who are up early to go running or start their days before their families. And I think about one of the morning blessings:

Who grants strength to the weary

While there are some people who make life seem effortless, for the rest of us, it can feel like a continuous and sometimes monumental uphill trek. It helps to think that we have an extra boost from above in even the mundane tasks like shaking off that early morning exhaustion.

Blessings on the Sabbath Candles

I'M GENERALLY A FAN of ritual and tradition. I'm not sure if it's because of my particular upbringing or background or simply because I like ceremonies, objects, or even foods to usher in a particular moment. On Friday nights, I can almost feel the world slowing down, or at least my world, as the sun sets and the Sabbath begins. Traditionally, 18 minutes before sunset, women light two or more candles to welcome the Sabbath, and they say the following blessing.

> *Blessed are you, Lord our God, sovereign*
> *of the universe, who has sanctified us with*
> *his commandments and commanded us*
> *to light the lights of Sabbath.*

Lighting Sabbath candles hails back to Sarah, who would light candles in the tent she shared with her husband Abraham. And for thousands of years, it's symbolized the moment when worries get shut out even for a few hours and families are granted peace and time for personal reflection.

Peace Be Upon You

*S*HALOM ALEICHEM IS a Hebrew greeting that means:

Peace be upon you.

The common response is *Aleichem Shalom,* or the reversed: "Upon you be peace." It sounds simple to say, but who wouldn't like a little more peace, or peace of mind, in their lives? On Friday nights there's a song called "Shalom Aleichem," which is traditionally sung by the heads of household upon their return home from the synagogue. The hymn is of unknown origin, but it's said to have been composed by the Kabbalists of Safed during the seventeenth century. The sentiment behind the song is lovely, as it's said to be a greeting to the two angels said to accompany people home from prayer on Friday night. Whether one takes things literally or metaphorically, it's nice to embrace the notion of wishing peace upon those who accompany us on life's journey.

A Woman of Valor

ONE OF THE MORE well-recognized Sabbath hymns is sung on Friday nights, and extols the virtues of the woman of the house. There's an interesting discourse about who actually composed this prayer, which originally appears at the closing of the Psalms. "A Woman of Valor" appears in the portion composed by Solomon, but was actually composed by Abraham as a eulogy for his wife Sarah. It's also a metaphorical prayer offering praise to the Sabbath Queen, the personification of the Sabbath:

> *An accomplished woman, who can find?*
> *Her value is far beyond pearls.*

This first line reminds me of my friend Peninah, whose name is the Hebrew word for "pearl." Peninah is both accomplished and down to earth, despite managing the finances of a major international corporation while her husband toils in academia. There's a Hebrew expression that also reminds me of Peninah, *K'shmah kayn hee*, "She is like her name."

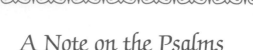

A Note on the Psalms

IKE SOME OF THE greatest works of literature, the Psalms have survived for thousands of years. And while it's considered a unified work, the Psalms actually were composed by different authors. The majority were written by King David and King Solomon, with contributions by Moses and even Adam, while others remain anonymous and unattributed. As with many prayers, individual chapters, verses, or the entire book can be taken as metaphor, poetry, life advice, or simply comforting words of wisdom passed down through the generations. While researching this book, I realized that there is so much modern wisdom and favored idioms that originated with these words. While I've included some universal favorites, I've also tried to include alternate insights and ideas.

She's Crafty

WHEN I WAS TWO YEARS OLD my mother opened her first boutique: a crafts shop crammed with rainbows of yarn and floss from floor to ceiling. And with the help of my mother, ever since I was old enough to tie knots in yarn, I've always been crafting or creating things. The prayer "A Woman of Valor" says:

> *She seeks wool and flax, and*
> *works with her hands willingly.*

Though it's had a resurgence of popularity recently, crafting is nothing new. It's the recognition of crafting as creation, and the virtue, if not divine pleasure, of making beautiful things out of nothing that's gained more recent favor. Best yet is sharing that skill and enjoyment with others. I once taught a total stranger on the F train to crochet, and we both felt the world was a slightly better place for our shared experience.

Know Your Worth

I T'S HARD NOT TO GET BEATEN DOWN by life sometimes. Professionally and personally, there are
people who seek to make themselves feel better by
belittling you and your skills; some people simply
feel it incumbent upon them to lift themselves up by
putting others down. In "A Woman of Valor," there's
a line that I never used to pay much attention to:

She knows that her merchandise is good.

There are so many lines within that prayer that are
better known. In rereading and studying the text,
I realized that, for all the praise it heaps on a very
traditional mother and wife, there are incredibly
modern messages in there as well. The woman
praised and portrayed within the prayer is both
strong and independent, and when she goes out
into her world, she has every confidence that her
offerings, whatever they may be, are impressive.

Be Kind (to Yourself)

I N READING THROUGH the prayer "A Woman of Valor," I was taken with one line that reads:

She opens her mouth in wisdom, and the lesson of kindness is on her tongue.

I was initially struck by the notion that someone who is truly wise is able to impart the lessons of kindness to others. And I thought about how cruel some kids can be and how important it is to actually teach them kindness. Then it hit me: We really need to learn to be kinder to ourselves. I, for one, would never be friends with someone who was as nasty to me as I sometimes am to myself. I beat myself up about my appearance and my weight, and my missed deadlines. And I yearn for the wisdom that will allow me to be as kind to myself as I try to be to others.

Beautiful on the Inside

I FIGURED I'D INCLUDE "A Woman of Valor" in this book, but never thought I'd include more than a mention. Because the way that I was raised, this is a prayer that was to be recited by a husband to his wife. And because I'm not married, this prayer never felt relevant or much appealed to me. One of the most famous lines in this prayer is:

Charm is deceptive and beauty is vain.

As someone who spent years as a celebrity make-up artist, I realize just how true that line is. I've worked with some of the more beautiful faces in the world only to realize that some of their insides were rotten. Then I could no longer see any beauty in them. Conversely, as a makeup artist, I was able to make anyone look beautiful, because I'd only focus on and highlight their best points, and the rest just faded away.

Shake off the Week

I LOVE FRIDAY NIGHTS, but perhaps not for the reasons that you might imagine. While my college friends counted down the hours until the weekend so that they could let loose, I counted down the hours until I could find myself again. There's a gorgeous prayer called *Lecha Dodi*, which translates to:

Come my beloved.

Many prayers are written metaphorically, but it always struck me as so endearing that the first prayer ushering in the day of rest is one that speaks sweetly and lovingly to what is ostensibly a day of the week. In this case, comparing the Sabbath to a bride and a group welcoming her into their fold. The prayer was composed by one of the mystics of ancient Safed in Israel, Rabbi Shlomo Alkabetz, who includes his name at the beginning of the prayer in an acrostic (a somewhat common signature in prayer composition). A lovely line that sums up leaving the week behind is:

Arise, now, shake off the dust.

Let Us Tell

Part I

ONE OF THE MORE SOBERING PRAYERS of the entire year is *Unetaneh Tokef*, "Let us tell," the beginning of the first line that continues *Kedushat Hayom*:

> *How utterly holy this day is.*

This prayer is said during the High Holy Days on both Rosh Hashanah and Yom Kippur. The prayer was composed by the eleventh-century sage Rabbi Amnon of Mainz, who felt he had to be punished for even pretending to think about renouncing his faith. He died a rather grisly death, and said this prayer in his synagogue on Rosh Hashana with his dying breaths. The lines compare the relationship between God and his people to a shepherd who counts and notices each member of his flock. The prayer goes through the options of what might befall a person during the year to come.

* * *

Part II

UNLIKE MOST NEW YEAR's celebrations, which are times for merriment, the Jewish New Year is about introspection and retrospection. It's believed that this is a time when God metaphorically inscribes into the book of life about the year ahead. *Unetaneh Tokef* goes through many options:

> *On Rosh Hashanah it is inscribed,*
> *And on Yom Kippur it is sealed.*
> *How many shall pass away and*
> * how many shall be born,*
> *Who shall live and who shall die.*

There's also a list of ways people might perish, and other food for thought. "Who will rest and who will wander?" I'm not sure why, but that line always gets me. Others include, "Who will become poor and who will get rich?" and "Who will be made humble and who will be raised up?" I think of not only myself, but also friends and even famous people whose lives have changed drastically in the past year, and I wonder about the year ahead.

Sweet Metaphors

ANCIENT PRAYERS ARE FULL of metaphor, and it's interesting to note that a lot of the practices and even foods follow suit. On Rosh Hashanah, the Jewish New Year, it's customary to eat an apple dipped in honey, as well as challah bread dipped in honey, to symbolize hopes for a sweet year. The short prayer that is said includes hopes that God will:

Renew for us a good and sweet year.

I love the fact that different foods and informal blessings have been added over the centuries. Some families eat tzimmes, a sweet carrots-stewed-with-fruit dish that comes with its own Yiddish-infused prayer for good things in the year ahead. Some traditions have morphed to the downright silly, including one my brother has shared about people combining a raisin and celery symbolizing hopes for a forthcoming raise in salary.

Oh, You Charming Teachers

P RAYERS DON'T HAVE TO BE all seriousness; sometimes there are parts or words or translations that simply make you smile. Psalm 45:3 states:

You are more handsome than other men.
Grace is poured upon thy lips.

In digging around a bit, I found Rashi's commentary tying this verse into someone who teaches people how to choose the right path. The endearing commentary states that when someone teaches others the right thing and right path, they are blessed with more charm than average. It reminded me of my father and sister, who were both teachers before segueing into other professions. They could literally enthrall a classroom of even the most unruly students. It also reminded me of one of my college professors, Professor Zlotnick, who was exacting in her pursuit of excellence. Haven't you had a teacher or professor that charmed you into changing your way of thinking?

Knowledge Is Freedom

I COME FROM A FAMILY of voracious readers. Some of my fondest memories involve us sitting and reading in companionable silence. While our family had the typical Shabbat customs, we also had one unique to us. Friday nights, my father would come home with two new books for each of us, and we had to choose one as our gift for that week. There were few things that I looked forward to as much as the end of our Friday night meal, when I'd see my choices for the week ahead. In rereading one of my favorite Sabbath hymns, *D'ror Yikra*, ("He Will Proclaim Freedom"), by tenth-century poet Dunash ben Labrat, I came upon a line that made me think of my childhood memories of Friday nights:

> *Know wisdom, that your soul may live.*

I'm forever grateful to my parents for instilling in me a love of reading and learning new things. What makes your soul come alive?

Join in Song

NOT QUITE PRAYERS, not quite chants, *piyutim* are a wonderful mixture of poetic language put to music. The Hebrew word *piyut* is said to originate from the Greek word for poet, and *piyutim* combines legend and history, mysticism, and shared experience. To be honest, I've never quite known how to define or identify them; I simply know them and feel them on some visceral level. *Piyutim* can include call and response, or soaring harmonies. I'm not sure if there actually is an equivalent in another language or culture that captures or encapsulates the rousing emotions that *piyutim* can embody in the singer and listener. The closest I've come, though, would have to be some of the pubs I've visited in Ireland. I remember in particular, a cold night in Belfast when I felt an immediate sense of warmth and camaraderie in listening to the ancient songs sung by a group of strangers joined in voice and our newly created shared history.

The Best of Friends

A LOVELY *PIYUT*, but not quite a prayer—more like a poem set to music—is *Yedid Nefesh*, which literally translated means "friend of the soul." The composer is debated, and it's sung at different times of the day or week, depending on tradition. It's a bit different from a traditional prayer, since the relationship between man and God is described as the warmest of friendships:

> *Your friendship will be sweeter than the dripping of the honeycomb and any taste.*

It's hard not to smile reading that. *Yedid Nefesh* reminds me of the novel *Anne of Green Gables*, where Anne describes true friends as "kindred spirits." I've definitely found a kindred spirit in my friend Ken. We live on separate coasts and I can't think of the last time we've seen each other face to face. But he's been there with me through the worst and he's rejoiced at my best. Who's your friend of the soul and why?

Blind Faith

I'VE MENTIONED THE NOTION of *piyutim*, or liturgical poetry or melodies that over the years have been integrated into prayer. *Anim Zemirot*, which means "I Will Sing Sweet Songs," is indeed one of the sweeter *piyutim*:

> *I make pleasant songs, and weave verses*
> *because for You my soul longs.*

This sounds like it might have been written by a lovesick suitor instead of by the 12th-century German Jewish mystic Rabbi Judah ben Samuel of Regensburg. Later lines, though, sound more like a declaration of blind faith:

> *I will recount Your glory, though*
> *I have not seen You. I describe You*
> *though I have not known You.*

My brother explains the unexplainable sometimes by likening it to radio waves. We can't see them, but for generations people have taken for granted that they're there, and somehow because they are, we hear music out of a box.

By Any Other Name

M ANY OBSERVANT PEOPLE don't spell out the name of God, for fear of disrespecting or destroying the paper it's written on. I know of people who spell it "Gcd" or "G-d." To take that notion a step further, some religious Jews might not fully pronounce or say God's name, instead saying *Hashem*, which means "the name," or mis-pronouncing elements, so the "H" or "hay" sound in Hebrew might be replaced with the hard "K" sound. So *Ein Keloheinu* ("None is like our God") might be pronounced *Ein Kelokaynu* in any time other than during prayer. This *piyut* uses four of the more common names for God:

> *There is none like our God, There is none like our Lord, There is none like our King, There is none like our Savior.*

It almost feels like when you love someone so much you can't help but shower them with endearments.

Make It Rain

YEARS BACK I WORKED with someone who would do his own approximation of a Native American rain dance around his desk when things were particularly slow around the office. Many cultures and faiths have variations of their own rain prayers, since their crops and food sources relied heavily on abundant rainfall. There's a neat blessing that switches its intent, depending on the time of year. *Morid Hatal* ("And the dew shall fall."), which is said in the *Shemoneh Esrei* prayer (the 18 blessings, though there are actually 19), beginning during the spring months is switched in the fall season to *Morid Hageshem*:

And the rain shall fall.

It's also a thoughtful prayer, since it's believed that the prayers for much needed rain are only invoked after all of the holiday pilgrims who were Oleh Regel or took the long journey up to ancient Jerusalem and the temple are safely back home and out of the rain by that point.

Spiritual Songs

ZEMIROT, THE HEBREW WORD for songs or hymns, are mostly associated with the Sabbath and holiday meals. While some are supposed to be recited at specific times of the day or at specific meals, others are just catch-all, feel-good tunes meant to add to the joyousness of the day. Some songs are based on chapters or verse from the Bible; others are taken from rabbinical texts or liturgy; still others are portions of poems or even folk songs passed down through families and throughout the centuries. Tunes vary, as does pronunciation or even language, which ranges from Hebrew to Aramaic to Ladino or Yiddish. While these songs aren't specifically meant to take the place of prayers, they generally are of an incredibly spiritual nature and cover topics including God, nature, the Diaspora, the Sabbath itself, family, and the happiness of the day of rest.

How Beloved

EVERY TIME I SEE the words *Mah Yedidot*, I can hear my father singing the melody in my head. While he's a man of many skills, my father isn't known for his voice. But whenever he sang this particular tune, my father would always mention the fact that he could always hear his own father singing this hymn in his own head. Whenever I have a hard time connecting to the melodies, stories, or prayers composed thousands of years ago, I think of my father's father teaching him this melody—and then wonder just how far back this particular tradition goes. In addition to traditional meals and melodies shared with family and friends, the Sabbath also brings with it special clothing. The line "Dressed in beautiful garments" reminds me of when I was really little and waited all week to wear my Sabbath shoes (black patent leather Mary Janes, in case you're wondering).

What Goes Up ...

WHILE I HOPE FOR GREAT THINGS and curse the fates when the really bad things transpire instead, I'm not particularly prone to jealousy. I figure that things tend to even out in the end. Not always, of course, but often enough. I marvel at the fact that there are people who earn millions of dollars each year simply by allowing TV cameras into their living rooms, but I digress. A Friday night melody, *Yah Ribon Olam* translates to "God Creator of the World." In discussing God's abilities, the hymn states:

> *Great and mighty are your deeds, humbling*
> *the proud and raising the humble.*

With apologies to Andy Warhol, it helps me to realize that sometimes 15 years of obscurity can be followed by 15 minutes of fame, and vice versa.

Lost in Translation

I HAVE MANY TALENTS, but translating texts between languages isn't my greatest skill. So I rely on traditional translations and try to interject my own gut reactions to certain wordplay. *Yom Shabbaton* is a wonderful Sabbath melody, and the words feel so pure and soar in the original Hebrew. In English, though, they feel a bit more grounded:

> *The day of rest should not be forgotten,*
> *its memory is like a satisfying aroma.*
> *On it the dove found rest, there*
> *shall rest exhausted ones.*

Well, that doesn't sound all that magical now, does it? But the thing is, the aroma in question refers to the incredible incenses burnt at the original temple; and the dove in question was the one who returned with an olive branch in its beak when Noah's ark settled on Mount Ararat. And I'm not sure there are words enough to convey leaving a hectic week for the peace of a day of rest.

A Note on Pronunciation

IF YOU'VE NEVER HEARD conversational Hebrew spoken, you might be put off the first time you actually hear the words aloud. To me, Hebrew sounds soothing and melodious and is quite literally my mother tongue. When I was little, my mother didn't speak to us in English because she didn't want us to pick up her (very charming) hybrid Romanian/Israeli accent. To the uninitiated, Hebrew words might sound guttural at best, or like someone trying to clear their throat in between uttering harsh consonants. Po-tay-toe/ Po-tah-toe, right? Well, actually, it is pretty close to something like that. Within the Hebrew language there are many different pronunciations and inflections, depending on level of observance, place of birth, religious observance, and so on. Much like the noted Bostonian or Southern accents, there are very marked accents placed on words, depending on family background and tradition. Most notable are the Hebrew letter *Taf*, which can sound either like an "S" or "T," and the Hebrew "Ch" found in words like Chanukah.

Playful, and
Not Quite a Prayer

WITH ALL OF THE SOMBER WORDS and meaningful moments in ancient prayer, you might think that it's all dark and serious. Well, it isn't. While most prayer is intended to be between a person and his or her maker, there's also so much that is shared joy and celebration. There are songs that are extremely spiritual but not quite prayers. They feel special, though, because they're only sung on the Sabbath. Imagine feeling that special about a song that could only be played on the radio on Tuesdays. One version of the classic song *Yom Zeh M'Chubad*, meaning "This Day Is Honored" has a very goofy call-and-response refrain in English. It makes no sense, but after the Hebrew words, some in the group add in "Whaddya say?" and the one singing the melody responds "This" and then repeats the verse. It's hard not to crack a smile when a room full of people alternate ancient texts with really silly verse.

It Will Be Good

JUST SO YOU KNOW, this isn't an ancient prayer, but more of a modern mantra that's been popularized and passed down for generations. When I first thought of writing a book about prayer, I thought about creating something that I might call, "Om My God," which could touch on the intersection and blending of different faiths and religions that share similar overall outlooks and philosophies. I still might write it someday. While this book contains mostly Old Testament or Hebrew Testament texts, I'd like to sprinkle in just a few texts that don't quite fit the more traditional mold. *Y'heya Tov* literally means:

It will be good.

It's a soothing way of saying that things might feel overwhelming now, but all will be well. And if you say it often enough, I suspect that you will start to believe it too!

This Too Shall Pass

L EGEND HAS IT that King Solomon commissioned a ring that would make a happy man sad and a sad man happy. The ring presented to him was engraved with either three words inscribed, *Gam Zeh Ya'Avor*, or the Hebrew initials Gimel (G) Zayin (Z) Yud (Y), meaning:

This too shall pass.

It's said that this ring was meant to remind him that the lowest of the lows would pass and things would return back to normal. But then again, that means that the best times would fade away as well. There are many variations of this saying, ranging from the words of Persian Sufi poets to Turkish folklore. I've uttered those words during both the lowest and highest points of my life. It helps me remember to savor the fantastic moments and know that the truly devastating ones will soon be the stuff of bad memories.

The Eighteen

Part I

IF YOU'VE EVER SEEN ANYONE sporting a curiously curlicued charm that they referred to as a *Chai* (Elvis Presley wore one), you'll know that they were wearing the Hebrew word for "life." Because of this gematria, or number play and symbolism, the number eighteen is considered a good luck number for Jews. The prayer of *Shmoneh Esrei*, which means "The Eighteen" for the eighteen original blessings in the prayer (there are now nineteen) is also called *Tefilat Amidah* or the "Standing Prayer," because it's said in complete silence and when standing very still.

Shmoneh Esrei is sort of the central part of daily prayer and begins with a blessing called *Avot*, which literally means "fathers," but is better translated to "ancestors" and offers praise for:

> *The God of Abraham, God of Isaac*
> *and God of Jacob.*

The belief wasn't diluted through the generations; each of the patriarchs had a close relationship and unwavering faith.

* * *

Part II

A CONTROVERSIAL ISSUE among practitioners of traditional Judeo-Christian-inspired faiths is whether or not they believe in the notion of reincarnation. It's a heavily debated issue, and there's no unilateral agreement or belief. In one section of the *Shmoneh Esrei* prayers are the *Gevurot* or strengths/powers. This section highlights God's abilities, including the power to heal the sick and resurrect the dead, referred to as *Mechayeh Matim*. Whenever I happen to say this prayer, I offer up a quick note of gratitude to Dr. Michael Grossbard and his staff at St. Luke's Roosevelt Hospital. Cancer felt like a living death to me, and Dr. Grossbard pushed, pulled, and bullied me back to health. And I'm not sure that I can ever repay the dedication and care of the eleventh-floor nursing team. I no longer wonder what might come next; I am simply grateful for those who helped give me another chance.

* * *

A Bit of Humor:
The Eighteen

Part III

I'M NOT SURE WHERE the belief originated that observant people have no sense of humor. From what I understood and was raised with, humor was an intrinsic part of faith. After all, if you couldn't laugh at the bleakest of circumstances, wouldn't you give up entirely? Rabbi Nachman of Breslov, a nineteenth-century Hassidic Rabbi, believed *Mitzvah Gedolah Lehiyot Besimcha*, meaning…

> *It's a great mitzvah [good deed or commandment] to be happy.*

Life is hard sometimes, and we need those moments of joy and laughter. I sometimes joke that I grew up with four mothers: my own and her three formidable older sisters. When my Tante Yitu died, I felt like the light had gone out of our family. Perhaps it's irreverent, but I always think of her during the *Shemoneh Esrei* prayer. There's a portion where God is referred to as *Somech Noflim*—he who "supports the fallen." *Somech Noflim* was also Tante Yitu's nickname for her bra.

* * *

Compose Your Own Prayer—Or Not:
The Eighteen

Part IV

A T THE TAIL END of the *Shmoneh Esrei*, there's a short section in which people are encouraged to add in their own personal beseechments and prayers. My oldest friend Blossom's mother was recently ill, and in recounting the story of meeting with her mother's surgeon, Blossom said that in her abject terror she drew a complete blank on what words she might even begin to use to pray for her mother. So, she started saying small bits of whatever songs, quotes, or Psalms that popped into her head. I've always felt that I could talk to God one-on-one and in my own words, and while I love the history and beauty of the language of prayer, sometimes I just want to pour my heart out. Blossom reminded me that sometimes the venerable words are there for us for when we just can't seem to find our own.

Prayers for Your Name Alone

D URING THE PART of the *Shmoneh Esrei* where you add in your own prayer, there's a custom to first say a verse or two that corresponds to your name. To clarify, immediately after the *Shmonah Esrei* prayers in most *siddurim*, or prayer books, there is a listing of *pesukim*, or verses that correspond to the first and last Hebrew letters of a name. For instance, one of my Hebrew names (I have two) is Rachel, but pronounced Rah-Chel (with the gutteral "ch" sound) and spelled with only three letters in Hebrew: *Raish, Chet*, and *Lamed*. I would look for the corresponding verse that begins with a *Raish* and ends with a *Lamed* and say that verse before launching into my own personal prayer. Because there can be several that correspond, people tend to choose the one that most resonates with them and then claim it as their own.

Claim a Prayer of Your Own

IT'S BEEN MANY YEARS since I read the novel *Inside, Outside* by Herman Wouk, himself a practicing Jew. I remember being struck by the way that the protagonist, an American Jew, had one name (and existence) by which he was known to the outside world, and another by which he was known to his observant family. While cultural mores have become so much more elastic over the past decade or so, I used to vigilantly keep my background private and observance or practices to myself. My *Inside* name is Ruchi, an affectionate diminutive of the Hebrew/Yiddish version of Rachel. I used to hate that name, but came to love it when I realized that it had a meaning of its own as well. *Ruchi* in Hebrew means "my soul" or "my spirit," and I feel a special connection to prayers mentioning my name. Are there any poems or prayers that you feel connected to more than others?

No More War

WHO AMONG US hasn't avoided turning on the nightly news or reading the morning headlines at some point? It seems like there's always someone in some part of the world who seems determined to wreak havoc. Perhaps I'm just a simple soul, but I wish it would all stop. I wish we could figure out a way to live peacefully with our neighbors—even the ones with loud barking dogs or drum sets. I wish that we could figure out a way to accept our differences instead of invading and destroying, or being forced to defend ourselves. Psalm 46:10 says:

> *He puts a stop to wars until the end*
> *of the earth; He will break the bow*
> *and cut the spear to pieces;*
> *He burns chariots with fire.*

From road rage to nuclear war, it would be comforting if indeed someone could put a stop to all the personal and global wars.

Eat Dessert First

WELL, NOT LITERALLY, but there's actually a general order, if a not hierarchy, of which blessings are said on which foods and the order in which they are said. Got it? And while some of you competed in spelling bees at school, I attended a fully bilingual half-day Hebrew/half-day English/ Secular studies all-girls school and competed in both spelling bees and *brachot*, or blessing bees. So if you're ever stuck for the proper blessing for tapioca pudding or empanadas, I'm your woman. One of the lesser-known aspects of blessings on food includes *chaviv*, the Hebrew word for favorite or most desired. So, if you've got a group of foods in front of you on which you'd say the identical blessing, you should have your favorite in mind. And feel free to send up an extra little prayer for those extra delicious dishes.

If You're Happy and You Know It

I'M GUESSING THAT the original intention of Psalm 47 was not to make me think of a popular children's song, but that's what happens when I read the second line:

> O clap your hands, all ye peoples; shout
> unto God with the voice of triumph.

I remember the sheer joy of being young enough that clapping my hands in unison with my classmates felt like a major accomplishment. Sometimes when you're at a concert or show and just appreciating the talents of others, there's incredible pleasure in being able to show your appreciation by clapping heartily along with hundreds, if not thousands, of strangers. It's amazing what a unifying effect one small gesture can have. Along those lines, not many professions have such clear ways of showing appreciation for great work. So perhaps take some time today to send an encouraging note to a friend, colleague, or supervisor who's improved your life in some way.

Tell the Story

THERE ARE SO MANY CULTURES that revere and pass down stories, legends, and prayers from generation to generation. Much like the Celtic storytelling tradition, a lot of ancient prayer and legend is repeated through the generations, and sometimes the origin is unclear or unattributed. Psalm 14:8, in speaking of a future victory, advises the listener to pay attention to the details:

In order that you may tell a later generation

I once heard of a Native American belief that a person isn't considered truly dead until the last person who knew a story about them dies as well. In cultures that value storytelling, rich history remains alive and vibrant instead of relegated to the faded pages of a forgotten tome.

Special Occasions Blessing

O NE OF MY FAVORITE BLESSINGS is hard to pronounce and harder to define. The blessing of *Shehecheyanu*, which literally translated means "Who has given life," is a blessing that celebrates the best, if not necessarily the most predictable occasions in life.

> *Blessed are You, Lord our God,*
> *ruler of the universe, who has*
> *granted us life, sustained us,*
> *and enabled us to reach this occasion.*

Which occasions? The really big ones like major Jewish holidays, including Yom Kippur or Chanukah. Life-changing events, such as the birth of a new child or purchase of a new home. Or quirkier ones, including eating a new fruit or wearing new clothing. You can even recite this blessing upon seeing a long-lost friend.

Life isn't always easy. And it certainly isn't predictable. And much in the way that we recite favorite lyrics to lift a bad mood ("The sun will come out tomorrow"), or tag lines from classic movies ("Tomorrow is another day"), sometimes prayers or blessings can serve a happier and higher purpose.

When you get through a tough time, or find the perfect dress for your high school reunion. When your kid aces her exams, or the damage to your car isn't as bad as you'd feared, send up a tiny blessing of thanks. It's amazing what acknowledging the small, good things can do for your outlook, mood, and long-term happiness.

Make It Meaningful

WE ALL STRIVE TO LIVE meaningful lives, but it can be hard to do for all of your waking hours. Sometimes you want to just unwind and think less noble thoughts. Psalm 49 is pretty grim and lists so many ways that life is short, saying that once we're gone, everything we've worked to achieve and all of our material goods are left for others. But living in an aggressively consumer-driven culture, it can be strangely comforting to muse on "Those who rely on their possessions and boast of their great wealth." In the book *Pirkei Avot* ("Chapters of the Fathers"), there's an expression I've always found to be true: *Marbeh Nichasim, Marbeh Da'agot*, which translates loosely to:

The more you have, the more you worry.

So, relax and enjoy the moment, and try to stop worrying about always accumulating more.

What Makes You Happy?

DO YOU EVER FEEL like you're just going through the motions in life? Then something monumental happens, and for better or worse you start to reevaluate everything you'd done or said or accepted as your norm until that point. In Chronicles Book 2, 29:30, there's a line discussing the worship of the ancient Levites and it says:

And they sang praises with gladness.

Granted, it was their job on the food chain of observance and service to, in fact, sing said praises but they were happy to do it—not forced, not coerced, but genuinely glad. Here's an odd thought: don't you even gain satisfaction from some of your own chores? It's illogical, but I love doing laundry and gain a tiny thrill when the house smells like freshly washed clothing. Sometimes the small things in life can bring you joy, even things that are considered hard work to others—like sustaining your belief, year after year.

Slander Put Another Way

SOMETIMES LOOKING AT WORDS or phrases differently can make things appear in an entirely new way. Case in point, in Psalm 50, there are lists of wrongdoings and pretty awful actions. There's one line, though, that really got to me:

Thou sittest and speakest against thy brother;
thou slanderest thine own mother's son.

I try hard not to speak ill of others, but it can be really difficult when gossip seems to be everyone's favorite pastime. In reading that line, I thought of the difficult relationship that even the closest family members may have. Siblings become alienated and stories are told. But when it comes right down to it, speaking ill of your brother is something of an insult to your mother. And if you take it one step further, on some level that means you're always insulting someone's mother by speaking badly of them!

Say It Once, Say It Loud

AN INTERESTING ASPECT of ancient prayer is all of the notes and instructions that come along with the individual prayers. Groups of prayers are gathered into something called a *Siddur* or prayer book, from the Hebrew word for "order." *Siddurim* (the plural of siddur) not only have the lists of prayers, but also instructions for before and after the prayer. So while some prayers are said out loud with the congregation, others are uttered to oneself. Unlike reading a traditional book, it's not only accepted to move one's lips while reading, it's also expected. People tend to shuffle or sway while praying as well, and believe it or not there's actually a unique word in Yiddish to describe the particular swaying common to prayer. It's known as "shockeling."

Forgiving Others: Psalm 51

Part I

DIFFERENT FAITHS HAVE RADICALLY different notions of forgiveness. While I tend almost universally to forget the bad things that people have done to me, there are some things that I deem unforgiveable. My Christian friends frequently seem shocked that I feel no urgency to forgive those who have wronged me. I understand that people are fallible, but one of the few universal purely black-and-white truths I've set for myself is that if someone intentionally harms me or those that I love, that person is no longer a friend. Psalm 51:8 says:

> *Behold, Thou desirest truth in the*
> *inward parts; make me, therefore,*
> *to know wisdom in mine inmost heart.*

That line reminds me how important it is to understand and trust yourself as you learn who deserves a second chance.

* * *

Forgiving Yourself: Psalm 51

Part II

C ONTINUING WITH THE THEME of forgiveness of
Psalm 51, something that I've had a harder time
with over the years is learning to forgive myself. I
felt so betrayed by my own body when it attacked
me from the inside. I felt hollowed out of hope and
like I had nothing to believe in. Verse 13 says:

> Do not cast me away from before You, and
> do not take Your holy spirit from me.

To me there was nothing sadder than feeling as
though I'd lost all of my faith and sense of self. I
think that one of the most important things that
we can learn as human beings is to be kind to ourselves and to strive to forgive ourselves and our
imperfections.

Tallit: Prayer Shawl

A TALLIT IS TRADITIONALLY a white woolen prayer shawl with black stripes and fringes on the four corners. Historically, a tallit was worn by a man during prayer, though the customs and styles have changed through the millennia. In our own times, you might see a woman wearing a hand-painted silk, fringeless tallit for her own prayer services. Tallit comes from the Aramaic word for "cover," and it's believed that a person wearing a tallit to pray is wrapping himself or herself away from external distractions and coming closer to God. There's no actual command for wearing a tallit, but rather the fringes attached to them to distinguish the wearer, since in ancient times everyone wrapped themselves in shawls of some sort or another. I always think of superheroes of faith when I see people wrapped in their tallitot.

Questioning and Still Believing

OKAY, YOU'RE THINKING, she's written a book about ancient prayer. She's likely pious to a fault and only talks about spiritual pursuits and hangs out with rabbis and priests and imams (Oh, my!). Not even close, gentle reader. My friends are diverse in nature. But if I stop to think about it, they have one common thread: they are all thinking folk. They don't simply accept everything that comes to them; they spend time delving into ideas and trying to understand how or why. Faith is a beautiful thing, but questioning and still wanting to believe, feels somehow greater. Psalm 53:3 says:

> *God looked forth from heaven upon the*
> *children of men, to see if there were any man*
> *of understanding, that did seek after God.*

What I took from this verse was that, as amazing as it is to have blind faith, it's a monumental accomplishment to seek and question and still believe.

Make Sure They're Listening

IN PSALM 54:4, the speaker is experiencing a particularly rough time and asks for help and guidance. At one point he says:

> Oh God, hearken to my prayer and incline
> Your ear to the words of my mouth.

Only then does he launch into a litany of complaints and requests. Before asking for help or pouring out your heart to someone, you need to make sure that they're actually open to hearing your request. A friend recently hurt my feelings, and while I almost immediately forgave her, I needed time to process things and I told her that. But she couldn't give me that time and instead kept writing and calling to try to make things better, which made me completely tune her out and completely defeated her original purpose. Don't ask for help unless you're sure that someone is listening to your plea.

I'd Fly Away

THERE ARE THOSE WHO view the Book of Psalms to be a wonderful book of poetry full of allegory and fables. And if that's your opinion and it brings you comfort or pleasure, that's your prerogative. Chapter 55:7–9 puts words (and wing) to feelings I think many of us have at particularly dark times:

> *Oh that I had wings like a dove!*
> *then would I fly away, and be at rest.*
> *Lo, then would I wander far off, I would*
> *lodge in the wilderness. I would hasten to a*
> *shelter from the stormy wind and tempest.*

When you're feeling blue, it helps to talk about your deepest feelings. And if it feels too hard to get those words out, try to imagine the freedom that might come from allowing your soul to take flight every now and again.

Get Outside of Yourself

AH, SELF-PITY—I'm not sure if it's the overwhelming despair or accompanying panic that's more overwhelming. Whichever it is, self-pity can make it hard to face even the most ordinary day. My mother calls it "the pity dance," when you just whirl around and around in a vortex of misery and try to involve others in your dark, bad place. It isn't pretty and it certainly doesn't make the situation any better. Psalm 56:4 says:

> *In the day that I am afraid,*
> *I will put my trust in Thee.*

The next time that you feel as though things might be spiraling out of control, try to find someone with the strength and clarity to help keep you from sinking into that pit. They don't have to help you figure everything out, just lend you a bit of their strength every now and again.

In Times of Trouble

INDEPENDENCE AND SELF-SUFFICIENCY are qualities that are greatly valued in our culture. We
aren't taught to be needy or to instinctively rely on
others, but who are we kidding? Having a support
network of trusted friends and loved ones is what
makes the difference between existing and fully
embracing our lives. In really rough times, though,
many people find or reclaim their faith. Psalm
57:2 says;

> *For in Thee hath my soul taken refuge;*
> *yea, in the shadow of Thy wings will I take*
> *refuge, until calamities be overpast.*

It's been said that there are no atheists in the fox-
hole, and finding comfort in prayer during the
hardest times doesn't make you weak—just human
and in need of a comfort that people can't always
provide.

When to Walk Away

I TRY MY HARDEST TO FIND the good in nearly everyone, and I feel dejected when I fail. In Psalm 58, the psalmist has some pretty harsh words to say about those tormenting him. He compares them to venomous snakes and says that even skilled snake charmers fail to reach them. Line 58:4 says:

The wicked are estranged from the womb;
the speakers of lies go astray as soon as
they are born.

I don't believe that people are born good or evil. I believe that circumstance and upbringing can have a lot to do with the way that a person turns out. I do believe, however, that sometimes you have to realize that no matter how hard you try, you'll never be able to reach them or help some people, and walking away helps you, which is in itself a noble goal.

Take the High Road

WHILE I'VE WORKED MOST of my adult life to become a better person, I have to admit something: It's not my intrinsic nature to be nice. In fact, time was that I enjoyed nothing better than razor-sharp verbal sparring with a worthy adversary. These days, though, I'd rather surround myself with positive feelings and people who make me feel good about myself. In Psalm 59, the psalmist offers repeated contrast between his enemies, who he says, "howl like dogs" and "swords are in their lips." In 59:17, he says:

But as for me, I will sing of Thy strength; yea,
I will sing aloud of Thy mercy in the morning.

Just because someone tries to bring out the worst in you, doesn't mean that you have to stoop to that person's level. It isn't always easy, but there's no greater feeling than being able to rise above someone intent on dragging you down.

Remember Your Own Strengths

IN READING THROUGH THE PSALMS composed by King David, it might be tempting to think him a weak man. He talks about his enemies and his fears and his frustrations. He speaks of his loneliness and betrayals and his deep need for help. In fact, in many ways, King David seems like a very modern man, in touch with his emotions, expressing them in verse and poetry and exposing his vulnerability to the world. But in Psalm 60, he reminds us of his victories as a great warrior and protector, and lists many of the battles he's waged and won in Aram-naharaim and Aram-zobah and Edom in the Valley of Salt, reminding the reader that he is, in fact, a brave warrior who believes his God to be his greatest strength. What's the bravest thing you've ever done?

Til the Ends of the Earth

I'M CONSTANTLY SURPRISED AT PEOPLE who go on vacations and seem to forget or discard their morals or ethics. It's not that I judge them, quite the opposite; if something is okay when you're away, why isn't it okay when you're at home too? The only person you end up fooling is yourself. Psalm 61:3 says:

> *From the end of the earth I call out to You*
> *when my heart becomes faint.*

My faith is the same no matter where I travel, though sometimes natural beauty or historical areas make me feel more connected. And I love knowing that no matter where I am or how alone I might feel, I'm always able to tap into that deep part of me and reach out for solace or comfort.

Talk It Out

I THINK WE ALL KNOW PEOPLE who keep their feelings bottled up inside. And sometimes when it gets to be too much for them, they explode in rage or sadness, or give the rest of us the silent treatment. There's something incredibly comforting about being able to pour out your soul to someone. There's something even more powerful about being able to pour out your deepest pain, wishes, and hopes to your God. There's no chance of judgment. You never have to regret having said the wrong thing or having to backtrack or take back your words. In Psalm 62:9 the psalmist says:

> *Trust in Him at all times, ye people;*
> *pour out your heart before Him.*
> *God is a refuge for us.*

I think that our relationship with God is what we make of it. And having a constant, non-judgmental and ever-present confidante is nothing to be minimized.

Sustenance

I'T'S SAID THAT PSALM 63 can be considered a prayer for professional success. And in reading the words, the imagery goes from starvation and privation to descriptions of great satisfaction. In Verse 2, the speaker says:

My soul thirsteth for Thee, my flesh longeth
for Thee, in a dry and weary land,
where no water is.

Later on in Verse 6, there are words of riches and sustenance:

My soul is satisfied as with marrow
and fatness; and my mouth doth
praise Thee with joyful lips.

There are so many different ways to find satisfaction and connection in life. In this case, the metaphors for food are easy to understand. For some people, faith fills certain vacuums and needs; for others, it can be a relationship with a close friend or a satisfying career or artistic pursuit. But we all need that kind of sustenance to feel whole.

Sticks and Stones

CONTRARY TO THE WISDOM of children's rhymes, sticks and stones aren't the only thing that can harm you. A well-placed jibe or cruel word can do the trick as well. Psalm 64:3 asks:

> *Hide me from the council of evil-doers; from the tumult of the workers of iniquity; Who have whet their tongue like a sword, and have aimed their arrow, a poisoned word.*

It feels in many ways like the culture of the "mean girl" has left the schoolyard and made its way into the working world and into adult friendships as well. It can be tempting to be part of the "in crowd"; but it's important to pay attention to what the insider clique says or does, and what joining up with them says about you.

Appreciate Nature

WHEN I WAS LITTLE, my mother would plant various seeds in our tiny-for-the-rest-of-the-world but gigantic-for-New York backyard garden. And in summer we'd gather the bounty in the form of delicious fruits and vegetables and fantastic flowers. Psalm 65 is full of luscious imagery; in Verse 10 the psalmist says:

> Thou hast remembered the earth,
> and watered her, greatly enriching her,
> with the river of God that is full of
> water; Thou preparest them corn,
> for so preparest Thou her.

And a bit later on in Verse 14:

> The meadows are clothed with flocks;
> the valleys also are covered over with
> corn; they shout for joy, yea, they sing.

We're so fortunate to have access to the most delicious and nutritious foods available, but sometimes it's important to remember where it all comes from, literally and figuratively.

Give Praise

MANY OF US FIND IT EASY to offer criticism when someone lets us down, but not to offer praise or compliments when they've done something amazing. Think about how often we grumble about everything from the way that our food is prepared at a restaurant, to the train being late, or the poor performance of a co-worker or colleague. In Psalm 66:3 the psalmist says:

> *Say unto God: "How tremendous*
> *is Thy work!"*

It strikes me as so endearing to think that people should be telling God: good job! But in essence that's what we do when we offer praise. Without even thinking about it, how many times have you said, "Oh my God," or "Thank God," or even "OMG?" Why not try to start thanking others for their help on a more regular basis as well. People need to feel appreciated, and it's easy to try to make it your second nature to do so.

When It Shines

I'M A HUGE FAN OF METAPHOR and symbolism in poetry and prayer. It helps me to understand some of the more arcane words or phrases that might feel somewhat awkward or out of place. I was a bit perplexed when I read the following words in Verse Psalm 67:2:

> God will be gracious to us and bless us;
> He will cause His countenance to shine
> with us forever.

As lovely as this image is, it felt confusing and didn't quite make sense to me. Rashi, a frequent commentator on the Psalms takes this to mean that the way God shows a shining countenance is by blessing us with rain and dew. When things seem unfathomable, sometimes it's easiest just to use words or expressions that make sense to us. And in essence, that's a lot of what the ancient prayers do: break down life cycles, events, and even nature into ideas that we can better relate to and understand.

Picture This

THERE ARE MANY COLORFUL expressions for losing control of one's emotions: being green with envy, or just plain feeling blue. Holly Golightly, the main character in *Breakfast at Tiffany's*, refers to anxiety as "the mean reds," and says, "Suddenly you're afraid, and you don't know what you're afraid of. Do you ever get that feeling?" We all get that feeling sometimes. In Psalm 68:3, the psalmist wants his enemies to disappear:

> *As smoke is driven away, so drive them away; as wax melteth before the fire, so let the wicked perish at the presence of God.*

It's hard to shake bad moods or take control of a situation when your emotions threaten to control your words. Trying to imagine a bad situation as a color or dissipating or evaporating feels like giving oneself an emotional time-out before responding angrily to that comment, text, or email.

When You're Tired of Crying

THERE ARE SO MANY REASONS that a good cry can be healthy for you, from clearing out debris from your eyes to eliminating toxins from your body, but I'm no doctor and this book is about prayer and not physiology. In an article in the *New York Times* a few years back, writer Benedict Carey wrote about tears as being, "The heart's own sign language, emotional perspiration from the well of common humanity." What an eloquent way of describing a physical reaction that taps directly into the heart when we're happiest and most heartbroken. Psalm 69:4 says:

I am weary of my crying; my throat is dried;
mine eyes fail while I wait for my God.

So indulge in a good cry when you need to and don't worry about letting your emotions get the better of you, but know when it's time to dry your eyes and move on as well.

It's Okay to Be Needy

MANY PARTS OF THE MOST famous ancient prayers sound incredibly familiar—because they are. Some portions appear in different sections of the Bible, while others reappear in Psalms or during the High Holy Days. Some lines are sung on sad occasions and then pop up again in commentary and in special readings. In Psalm 70, the psalmist has many of the same words and nearly identical themes of previous Psalms, asking for help, asking that his enemies are shown up for what they are. Verse 6 says:

> *But I am poor and needy;*
> *Oh God, make haste unto me.*

Our culture tends to view neediness as a negative trait, so we build artificial barriers in our relationships and pretend to be fine when we're not. It's hard to be vulnerable, moreso to admit it, and even more difficult to repeat that need.

Form Your Own Family

A S PREVIOUSLY MENTIONED, portions of Psalms appear in different prayers. One of the more poignant prayers of the High Holy Days uses nearly identical language to Psalm 71:9:

Cast me not off in the time of old age;
when my strength faileth, forsake me not.

I can so clearly see my mother in the synagogue sobbing as the congregation sang these words. We all hope that we will spend our lives with people that we love, and that as we age, we will continue to support and care for each other. But sometimes people fall out of love and families lose touch. And marriages that were intended to last forever break up and deepest bonds are broken. The word "family" can mean so many things, and it can be the people that you choose to call family who will be there for you always.

Sign Your Name

IT CAN BE HARD to take credit for personal and professional accomplishments, especially for women who, for better or worse, are used to being the ones to bolster everyone else in their lives. Painters get to sign their names on their canvases, authors get to have their name on the covers of books, but what about more esoteric accomplishments? I regularly hear from friends, colleagues, and clients who get frustrated when their bosses or co-workers take credit for their work. And it can be debilitating to see others benefiting from your best efforts. Psalm 72 ends:

> *The prayers of David the son of*
> *Jesse are ended.*

It seems a fitting coda to such an important body of work. It's important to credit others for their accomplishments, and also to take credit when credit is due.

Take Counsel

MANY PEOPLE BELIEVE that specific Psalms can bring inspiration or guidance during certain life events. And as you read through the chapters, you'll start to notice patterns. Some chapters discuss journeys, and others address loneliness or illness. And while some are simply beautiful prose, others offer inspiration or empathy. Psalm 73 is thought to offer strength while facing legal battles or court cases, and Verse 24 says:

Thou wilt guide me with Thy counsel, and
afterward receive me with glory.

This helps one to realize that it's a good idea to get outside of your own head sometimes. Ask others for advice before making big decisions, and in the really potentially life-changing moments, seek professional counsel.

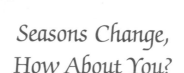

Seasons Change, How About You?

PSALM 74 COVERS LOTS of ground and topics. There's talk of enemies and the evil that they do and speak. And there's some wonderful imagery as well, about God saving his people from all means of destruction—including sea monsters, no less. And then there's a line that made me think about our ability to reinvent ourselves after each great victory or loss. Psalm 74:17 says:

> Thou hast set all the borders of the earth;
> Thou hast made summer and winter.

It's one of those lines that almost gives one pause. The borders are set and yet within them, there's orderly and regular change and upheaval: time for renewal after a long cold winter, and time to rest and renew during those harsh colder months. Consider taking a cue from nature every now and again and learn how to start anew and re-create yourself on a regular basis.

Sometimes You're Up

I F YOU JUDGED THE STATE of the world based on people's updates on their social networks and holiday cards, you might assume that everything is always rosy. The kids are doing great in school, and everyone has an incredibly fulfilling job, eats out at the most delicious restaurants, and takes dream vacations to hard-to-pronounce destinations. Reality, of course, is an entirely different issue. Some times are better, some are worse. And comparing ourselves to everyone else can only serve to minimize the really great things in our own lives. In Psalm 75:8, the psalmist says:

> *For God is judge; He putteth down one,*
> *and lifteth up another.*

The only consistent thing in life is inconsistency, so make sure to enjoy the really good times, because those memories will see you through the pretty crummy ones.

No Matter Their Weapons

PRAYER CAN SHORE UP your strength when you feel that you need an extra boost. For instance, my book files weren't loading earlier, and instead of freaking out, I kept thinking, "Please let them open. Please let them open,"—until they opened. I don't fool myself into thinking my good thoughts encouraged my files to open, but it did give me a way of channeling my panic into positive thoughts. Psalm 76 has a host of commentary by Rashi and others on one particular word contained within Verse 4:

> *There He broke the fiery shafts of*
> *the bow [arrows]; the shield, and*
> *the sword, and the battle.*

According to the commentary, the use of the word for arrow, *rishpay*, has a unique presentation. And we're to learn from this, that these were no ordinary arrows, but perhaps were controlled by evil forces. By putting positive thoughts and prayer into the world, you could be fighting forces you didn't even know you've been up against.

Speak Up

I'T'S BEEN SAID THAT PEOPLE fear public speaking almost as much as they fear death. And one of the hardest things for people to do is speak up when they need help. Even more importantly, people seem to feel ineffectual in knowing how to address injustice in their lives, much less on a global level. In Psalm 77:2, the psalmist says:

> I will lift up my voice unto God, and cry;
>   I will lift up my voice unto God,
>   that He may give ear unto me.

Though prayer is important on so many levels, there are times when people need to hear your words as well. Just as there are times when it's more prudent to keep quiet, there are other times when you need to overcome your fear or shyness and make your voice heard.

Choose Words Wisely

YOU FINALLY WORKED UP the nerve to confront someone about something they've done or said, or should be doing or should be saying, only to notice that your words have had no impact at all. Worse, the person resents your input. Psalm 78 includes a dark and winding tale full of past history and misdeeds, but Verse 2 begins:

I will open my mouth with a parable; I will utter dark sayings concerning days of old.

Instead of potentially alienating the listener with words of doom and gloom, the speaker immediately tells his listeners that the words are neither addressed to them nor about them, but are merely about times past. My mother is fond of a Yiddish saying: *Tuchter Deer Zug Ich, Schneer Deech Mein Ich,* which means, "Daughter, I'm talking to you, but I mean daughter-in-law." There's nothing wrong with finding creative ways to get a message across without offending or alienating anyone.

Let It Go

In any close relationship, be it parent and child, sister and brother, lovers, or close friends, there are going to be moments where one party upsets the other. And these bad feelings can feel magnified until they're either brought out in the open in the healthiest way possible, or explode into a firestorm of emotion or long-buried negativity. In Psalm 79:5, the psalmist says:

> *How long, O Lord, wilt Thou be angry for ever? How long will Thy jealousy burn like fire?*

Wouldn't it be amazing if we could actually put a timetable on bad feelings? Such as: *Your husband will fume until Tuesday, the fourth at 9:52 a.m., at which time he will morph back into his formerly loveable self.* But life doesn't work that way. And if you love someone, you'll try to move forward together after more tempestuous shared moments instead of constantly reminding each other of past pain.

The Best of the Worst

ANCIENT TEXTS ARE RICH with deep layers of commentary. For the purposes of this book, however, I prefer to limit them and instead include shorter messages applicable to modern life. Psalm 80:6 has a particularly interesting sentence that's worth exploring on a deeper level:

> *Thou hast fed them with the bread of tears, and given them tears to drink in large measure.*

It seems a simple enough metaphor about being full of sadness. Yet biblical sages say these tears refer to the three tears shed by Esau, twin brother of Jacob, who wept to his father Isaac in Genesis 27:34: "He cried with an exceeding great and bitter cry." Esau's three tears merited him the ability to earn a living through his sword, meaning he was literally fed with the bread of his tears. More than that, he warranted a reference in the Book of Psalms. While Esau was considered the quintessential biblical bad guy, even he was not too far gone for redemption.

The Dangers of Being Judgmental

TRYING NOT TO BE JUDGMENTAL of others is a struggle many of us share, and one that is magnified by our very connected and interconnected world. In the not-so-old days, it was easy to lose touch with people and remain unaware of every element of their lives. But what was once private is now almost all available for public consumption, and it can be all too easy to pass judgment on everything from people's choices of a life partner to their politics to innocuous things like their children's names or wardrobes. Psalm 82:1 says:

In the midst of the judges, He judgeth.

The Psalm itself is discussing the judges of the ancient Israelites and is gently chiding them and reminding them that while they may reign supreme over people, they themselves are being judged by a higher power. It's pretty potent stuff, and an excellent reminder.

Once in a New Moon

Y OU KNOW HOW SOME DAYS tend to bleed into the next with the same old boring routine? Kids. Parents. Work. Doctor's appointments. Rent. Mortgage. Lather, rinse, repeat. And then the wonderful calendar dates show up—birthdays, holidays, anniversaries, days that you count down to and plan for—and all too soon they're gone for another year. In the Hebrew, or lunar calendar, there is a reason for celebration at least once a month. Psalm 81:4 says:

> *Blow the horn at the new moon,*
> *at the full moon for our feast-day.*

The first day(s) of the month are referred to as *Rosh Chodesh*, or the "head of the month," which comes complete with its own prayers. In addition to existing holidays, the beginning of the new month is considered a minor holiday. In fact, the month of *Cheshvan*, which usually coincides with November on the secular calendar, is referred to as *Mar Cheshvan*, or "bitter *Cheshvan*," because in an anthropomorphized way, the month is thought to be sad since it contains no holidays.

* * *

Part II

THERE ARE SPECIFIC PRAYERS said to usher in the new month as well. The *Kiddush Levana* or "Sanctification of the Moon," is one of those beautiful and almost spooky services. The prayer includes these lovely words:

> *Praise them, sun and moon;*
> *praise them, all bright stars.*

This prayer is traditionally said only by men in a quorum, and said over the sliver of the new moon and on cloudless nights only. It's a primal feeling to be able to connect with the rhythm of the moon and the tides, and it's fun to have a reason to celebrate every month. Why wait until the traditional calendar dates for celebration? Find a new reason to celebrate life at least once each month!

Do the Right Thing by Your Employees

TOWARD THE END of Chapter 5 in *Perek Shira*, the Song of Creation, there's a reference to the "fox's prayer." Foxes are generally known for their cunning and wit, and yet the fox says these words originally found in Jeremiah 22:13:

> *Woe unto him that buildeth his house by unrighteousness, and his chambers by injustice; that useth his neighbor's service without wages, and giveth him not his hire.*

Most parables and fables involving foxes have them stealing grapes or triumphing over their fellow inhabitants of the animal kingdom. It's doubly interesting, then, to note that it's a fox that ostensibly cautions against building your home or business by nefarious methods.

In modern times, there's been a proliferation of businesses and enterprises that try to convince skilled individuals to give out their work and hard labor for free. But even the cunning fox knows that you have to pay people for their labor and appreciate their talents and best efforts. It's just the right thing to do.

Not Lip Service

YOU KNOW THOSE THINGS that are drummed into you as a kid and then forgotten? Those very specific words that trigger memories that almost make you shudder decades after the fact? *Kavanah* or "intent" is one of those words—but I really wish it weren't, because as an adult I clearly see the beautiful concept the word embodies. But as a child, my Hebrew teachers practically hissed at us to *Daven* with *kavanah*. "Pray with intent," they said. (*Daven* is the Yiddish word for "pray," but it's almost universally understood and used in modern language.) But what child of quasi-privilege truly understands the meaning behind those words? As a child, the closest I could get to making it meaningful was simply repeating the centuries-old words. As an adult, I think that my *kavanah* frequently means more than my actual words. Because I've lived and I've suffered, I know exactly what I'm praying for.

Aramaic and Greek in Prayer

WHILE THE BULK of this book covers the mostly Hebrew ancient prayers found in the Old Testament, or Hebrew Testament as it is now commonly known, it also includes a soupçon of other cultures as well. Phillip Katz, who is a professor of World Religions in the Workplace at Manhattan College, helped me better grasp some subtleties in both the religious and cultural implications of prayer and the languages most commonly used. While ancient Aramaic was once a common language of the Semitic people, it is now relegated to the more ancient prayers, texts, and commentaries. Historically, as the Israelites were taken down into slavery in Egypt, their languages expanded somewhat to include the Greek commonly spoken by the Egyptians. And while many prayers, most especially the apocryphal, or those composed after the cutoff date that delineates the Old and New Testaments, are in Greek, it should be noted that at the time, and to many religious scholars, they were as relevant as the more commonly used Hebrew prayers.

Keep the Momentum Going

I'M ALWAYS DISCOVERING and rediscovering favorite and unexpected gems in the ancient prayers. And I'm not even sure how I missed the fact that the expression popular in the U.K. about going from strength to strength, originated with Psalms. In describing the faithful, Psalm 84:8 says:

They go from strength to strength.

So we've got the origin down, but what about the intent? Newton's First Law of Motion is the one that says that a body in motion stays in motion, and one at rest, well, it isn't about to go anywhere. I'd like to think that more than simply praising someone for their strengths, we can take it a step deeper and imagine that it also means not to be content to rest on your laurels. I believe that we all have the ability to make amazing things happen—as long as we keep moving forward instead of being content with just good enough.

A Friend in Need

WE ALL HAVE FRIENDS for different parts of our lives. Some friends share the fun, while others share the burdens. Some friends are there through thick or thin, while others flit in and out over the years. My sister used to teach preschool and said there were some kids who only befriended others right before and only for their birthdays. In this way, they could sit right next to the birthday girl in every picture and be the one getting the rose from the birthday cake. In Psalm 86:7, the psalmist says to God:

> *In the day of my trouble I call upon Thee;*
> *for Thou wilt answer me.*

This sounds to me like the friends who are there when you need them most, unquestioningly, unflinchingly and without judgment. Which type of friend are you?

Favorite Places

DID YOU EVER VISIT A PLACE for the first time only to feel deep in your soul that you'd somehow been there before? Or maybe you're one of those people who relates most closely to a culture that isn't the one you were born or raised with. I felt that way the first time that I visited Scotland; for my friend Blish, it's Japan. Psalm 87 is very short and slightly confusing. It talks about Jerusalem as a capital of poetry and learning while comparing it to the other famous and popular cities of the time. I've been to Jerusalem many times over the years, and it never ceases to take my breath away to be at such an epicenter of so much faith and history. I can only imagine what Jerusalem must have been like at the height of its glory. Or as the psalmist concludes in Verse 7:

> *All my thoughts are in thee.*

Show Some Appreciation

I'M DEBATING JUST HOW to phrase this, but my cousin Isaac is not particularly known for his prowess as a public speaker. And yet I regularly refer back to a speech he gave some years back at a family event. Isaac is much older than I, and was reminding his newlywed niece to always remember the concept of *Hakarat Hatov*, which translates literally to "Appreciation of Good." But *Hakarat Hatov* is more about never taking the good things in your life for granted, and always remembering to be grateful for what you have. In Psalm 88:13 the psalmist says:

> *Shall Thy wonders be known in the dark? and*
> *Thy righteousness in the land of forgetfulness?*

It's a good reminder always to remember to thank those who do something nice for you. And don't ever take the good things for granted.

Don't Carry a Grudge

L IKE MOST PEOPLE, I have favorite or familiar Psalms and prayers, and then there are others that are familiar enough, but far from the top of my list. Psalm 89 is long and goes on for a while, and in it the psalmist seems to dredge up a lot of past hopes and resentments. There's talk of ancient enemies and battles won and lost. And then Verse 48 says:

Oh remember how short my time is.

This pithy sentence clears away some of the clutter from earlier in the Psalm and puts everything into perspective. Life is very short. And despite the residual pain felt from long-ago grudges or slights or heartaches, sometimes it's important just to let those bad feelings go. People tend to tune you out after a while if you keep raging and raving about the same thing constantly. And you can't change history—but you can change attitude.

Do Good Work

THE ANCIENT TEXTS are full of stories of people punished for wrongdoing, and while I try to focus on the loving, generous spirit of God, it's sometimes hard to tap into a story or lesson without dealing with the fire and brimstone aspects as well. It's said that Adam was the reason that mankind is cursed to have to work to earn a living. Genesis 3:19:

> *By the sweat of your brow*
> *you will eat your food.*

Some of us are fortunate enough to have found professional pursuits that nourish our souls instead of draining them. I'd like to think that the conclusion of Psalm 90 is about inspiring us to take pride in any work that we do and hope that if we're very fortunate, it will be blessed from above:

> *Let the graciousness of the Lord our God*
> *be upon us; establish Thou also upon us*
> *the work of our hands; yea.*

Out of the Mouth of Babes

I'LL ADMIT IT: I'm as surprised as you are to realize that this commonly used idiom has its origins in Psalm 8. In this case, though, it's almost to illustrate the innate genius of even babies, or especially babies, to recognize the greatness of God:

> Out of the mouth of babes and nursing
> babies hast Thou founded strength.

There are countless statistics to how many times a day babies laugh compared to adults. Their thoughts haven't been clouded by life or pain or experience. They're able to see things clearly, sometimes more clearly than the adults around them. Sometimes when we're afraid that we've lost our faith, the most important thing we can do is to take a giant step back from everything we thought we knew and simply go back to basics.

Take Comfort in Your Faith

F AITH MEANS DIFFERENT THINGS to different people. For some it's the unwavering belief in the religion that they were raised in from birth. For others it means carrying on a simple tradition or speaking a language or dialect passed on through generations. For still others, it means simply getting out of bed every morning and continuing a routine, and not giving into the sadness that can sometimes overwhelm them. In Psalm 94:19 the psalmist declares:

> *When my cares are many within me,*
> *Thy comforts delight my soul.*

I believe that faith is what you make of it. So learning to love again might mean that you have great faith in the good in the world. Or planting tulip bulbs in the fall means that you have faith that you will make it through a cold hard winter and will see another springtime.

Learn from the Past

ONE OF THE HARDEST lessons to learn in life is that we do, in fact, have to learn lessons—and frequently the hard way, through painful experience. We aren't simply born perfect, compassionate people, but have to work on ourselves to become more enlightened versions of our former selves. In addition to comfort, prayer can also help expedite some of those lessons. In Psalm 95:10, the psalmist says, in the words of God:

> *I wearied with that generation, and said*
> *it is a people that do err in their heart,*
> *and they have not known my ways.*

The generation past wasn't intentionally wrong; they simply didn't know his ways. It's important to pay attention to those who came before you and learn from both their successes and mistakes. There are no shortcuts in life, but sometimes there are great lessons to be learned.

Change Your Tune

I FREQUENTLY FIND MYSELF obsessed with covers, or newer versions of songs that were once my favorites and are now sung by different artists. The words or music might be the same, yet a new voice and arrangement makes everything different and new again. Psalm 96 begins:

Oh sing unto the Lord a new song;
sing unto the Lord, all the earth.

But are there really any new tunes that can be sung? Ecclesiastes says, *Ein chadash tachat hashemesh*, which means, "There is nothing new under the sun." Yet, we constantly hear new songs that capture our attention, or read new works of literature that become classics for our own time. When there's nothing new to say, we have to challenge ourselves to find new ways to say it. When daily routine or even prayer feels a bit stale, perhaps it's time to look deeper and find new meaning within the words and within ourselves.

The Lord's Prayer: Universal Themes

WHILE THIS BOOK FOCUSES almost exclusive-ly on the ancient prayers found in the Old Testament, I'd like to include a few prayers from other sources as well. Phillip Katz, a professor of world religions, said that of all the Christian prayers, The Lord's Prayer has universal themes that can be understood and applied by nearly any-one who believes in a higher power. Also known as "Our Father," the prayer has many similarities to the ancient Hebrew texts as well. One line that always stands out for me is:

> *Forgive us our trespasses, as we forgive*
> *them that trespass against us.*

Forgiveness is such a personal issue, and it helps to try to think of all of the wrongs we do when we withhold forgiveness from others. As an interest-ing aside on the universality of these words, even Hobbits could relate to this prayer; J.R.R. Tolkien translated The Lord's Prayer into Quenya, the fic-tional language of *The Lord of the Rings*.

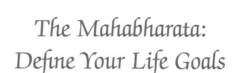

The Mahabharata:
Define Your Life Goals

M Y FATHER JOKINGLY referred to himself as my research assistant during the writing of this book, and kept emailing me suggestions and prayers to include. And at one point, he said I couldn't write a book about ancient prayer without including the *Mahabharata*, one of the two major epics of classical Sanskrit literature, which translates to the "Great Epic of the Bharata Dynasty." Composed by the Hindu sage Vyasa in about 450 BCE, The *Mahabharata* contains 18 volumes, 100,000 verses and about 1.8 million words. Book 12, known as "The Book of Peace," contains the four *purusarthas*, or main qualities most sought after by man, which are: *Dharma* or the rightful order of things; *Artha*, which are material needs; Kama, or pleasure; and *Moksa* or liberation. Wouldn't life be so much easier if you could so simply and succinctly define your own goals, hopes and outlooks?

Jonah:
Out of the Pit of Darkness

WHILE MOST SCHOOLCHILDREN can tell you the story of the prophet Jonah, who was swallowed by a whale, they probably don't understand the subtleties and metaphors of the tale. Of Jonah trying to outrun his destiny by sailing far away. Of God creating a tremendous tempest at sea that threatened the lives of his shipmates. Of Jonah encouraging his shipmates to cast him out, the seas subsequently calming, and Jonah being swallowed by a whale. And from that dark pit, quite literally the belly of the beast, Jonah found the words to pray for forgiveness and release. Jonah 2:3 says:

> *I called out of mine affliction unto*
> *the Lord, and He answered me;*
> *out of the belly of the nether-world*
> *cried I, and thou heardest my voice.*

Sometimes you have to sink pretty low before you can start asking for help. And hopefully, someone will be there to help lift you out of that bad place.

Prayer Before Writing

WHEN MY FATHER TOLD me that he'd remembered a great prayer to recite before writing, naturally I assumed it would be one composed by some great rabbi in days of yore. I was wrong. Saint Thomas Aquinas was a thirteenth-century Catholic priest and philosopher who composed a prayer to be said before writing or preaching that included these words:

> *Make my intellect sharp, my memory clear,*
> *and my words eloquent, so that I may*
> *faithfully interpret the mysteries*
> *which You have revealed.*

While I utter words of prayers and blessings on a daily basis by rote, and despite the fact that I've spent decades studying ancient texts, I'm certain that my interpretations and observances won't please everyone. My hope though, is that at the very least, you find at least one bit of inspiration or food for thought within these pages. Other than that, all I can hope is that I've added some support or optimism to your day.

Idol Worship

SOMETHING I'VE ALWAYS HAD a hard time understanding or relating to is the idol worship prev-
alent in ancient faiths. And yet in our own times,
I've been charmed by family altars at the homes
of friends, or intrigued by small altars to Buddha
with oranges or incense or other offerings. Psalm
97:7 says:

> *Ashamed be all they that serve graven images,*
> *that boast themselves of things of nought.*

Perhaps our own generation's challenge with idola-
try is more in the obsessive worship of celebrities
and designer labels. Don't get me wrong, I'm a huge
fan of pop culture and I love stylish clothing and
accessories. I just don't revere them above all and
denigrate people who can't afford to drape themselves exclusively in the imprint of the designer du
jour. Perhaps the lesson here is not to worship arti-
fice and exteriors over people or institutions truly
worthy of our admiration.

I Believe

WHEN I WAS YOUNGER, I never questioned my faith. It was instilled in me before I had memories of my own and reinforced on a daily basis. As I grew up and faced outside influences and challenges, my faith sometimes wavered. And when I faced a life-threatening illness, for a while there my faith disappeared completely. Little by little, I've been able to rediscover the things that I found most beautiful about the faith I was raised with and hope someday to pass on to my own future children. To be honest, not everything always makes sense to me. But I'm okay with believing simply because, for thousands of years, the people who came before me did just that. *Ani Maamin*, or "I Believe" is a haunting song based on the words of Maimonides in his 13 Principles of Faith, and part of a larger prayer. Sometimes simply believing for the sake of believing can be both comforting and empowering.

Love Your Neighbor

A S A VERY YOUNG GIRL, and before I could even understand the notion of prayer, I wholeheartedly embraced the songs we were taught in preschool (and can probably still sing all of them). These became mantras and declarations of our nascent and untested faith. One of the first songs I was taught and sang on a daily basis, along with the line or two of prayer that I already knew, was from Leviticus 19:18b:

> *Rabbi Akiva said:*
> *Love your neighbor as yourself.*

It's easier sometimes to learn these huge lessons when the song versions are already so embedded in one's psyche. Along with the golden rule and other informal homilies, this became a way to remember to always treat others in exactly the way that you wanted to be treated.

Toot Your Own Horn

I HAVE NO IDEA of the origin of the song "Blessed Is the One," which is sung on the Sabbath; and I am certain that there are those who would argue with me that technically it isn't even a prayer. I beg to differ. If prayer is composed of thanks and praise and wishes encapsulated into words, shouldn't we have one that pithily praises the one doing the praying for a change?

> *Blessed is the one who trusts in the Lord,*
> *whose confidence is in Him.*

It isn't easy to believe steadfastly in anything, most especially in a world that seeks to mock or marginalize people of faith. So whether you believe in God or nature or the inherent goodness of mankind, I think you deserve your own prayer and moment of glory. Go, you!

Blessed Rest

I WASN'T ALWAYS THE MELLOW SOUL that I am now. There was a while there—when I was working a full-time job and going to college at night—that late nights and weekends were spent in pursuit of fun. And it was fun, believe me. But after a while, it became numbing and draining and depressing. Imagine that. Being driven to do and experience and find the next big, fun thing made me feel empty inside. There's a gorgeous Sabbath hymn, *Baruch El Elyon*, which is the start of every stanza and means "Blessed is the exalted God":

> *Blessed is the exalted God who gave rest for our souls, a respite from calamity and woe.*

It's hard for me to believe that I once resented the stringencies of the Sabbath. One of the greatest gifts I've ever received was one I choose to experience on my own on a weekly basis. Shutting off from the rest of the world and relaxing, rejuvenating, and nourishing my weary soul. For me, the Sabbath adds as much as it shuts out.

All Are Welcome

IT IS TRADITIONAL to begin the Passover seder [the lavish meal marking the beginning of Passover] by chanting the Aramaic words *Kol Dichfin Yesei V'Yeichal; Kol Ditzrich Yesei V'Yifsach*, which are part of a slightly longer prayer:

> *All who are hungry let them come and eat; all who are in need, let them come and celebrate.*

Hospitality is one of the tenets of many religions, and in the ancient texts the Sabbath and celebration days were considered a time when guests were a given. Sure, most of us include family and friends at our Thanksgiving or Christmas dinners, but what about the notion of absolutely anyone being welcome?

In a family of house-proud women, my Aunt Judy is one of the more fastidious housekeepers I know. Her home is pristine, without a nicknack or tchotchke out of place at any given time. I recall one Passover when she and my uncle AJ invited a local homeless man to their seder. They are known for their community outreach among those less fortunate, but the homeless man, Mendel, was rather difficult to be around, so much so that people crossed the street to avoid passing him. My uncle took him under his wing and arranged for him to have his first bath in more than a year. He bought him a new suit and seated him as a guest of honor among his children and grandchildren. In this way, he was making a living example of making all welcome. I'm not sure that I could ever reach that level of hospitality, but anytime I grumble about guests overstaying their welcome, I think of the great lengths that others go to making others welcome in their own homes.

Is Your House in Order?

Too many people find themselves simply going through the motions of daily life. They wake up every day and fall into the same routine as the day that came before. They count down the hours until they can go home and unwind and stare at the TV or computer screen for a few hours until they go to sleep, and then they wake up again the next morning and do the exact same thing again the next day and the day after that one, trying to remember where the joy went or, more than that, the passion that once led them from one point to the next. Psalm 101:2 says:

I will walk within my house
in the integrity of my heart.

Take a look around. Is your home a refuge or a glorified media room? Can you reclaim a ritual, hobby, or passion that added some life to your life?

Be More Accepting

BECAUSE I GREW UP in a household in which several languages were spoken, I'm used to hearing snippets of one language and answering in another, and then hearing a response in yet another language. And in reading through the Hebrew texts, I only just realized that I also do a quickie transliteration in my head and compare my version to the accepted translations. Psalm 102:18 has a line with a few words that are defined differently. My translation would be:

> *When he hath regarded the prayer of the lonely one, and hath not mocked their prayer.*

I say "mocked" instead of the frequently used "despised." It can be brutal to open up to someone, much less pour your heart to them. And I think that the cruelest thing someone can do is mock your best efforts. This verse reminds us not to ridicule those who come to us with hearts open and exposed.

Remember Shared History

A T 45 VERSES, PSALM 105 is pretty long. It begins by offering praise to God, and along the way goes through a brief version of the history of Abraham, Isaac, Jacob, and Joseph, from the earliest covenants between God and the forefathers to Joseph's descent into slavery. But wait, there's also mention of Moses and Aaron and the 12 plagues in Egypt before the Psalm circles back to talk about God's covenant with Abraham yet again. In any long-term relationship, there are going to be high points and low points and moments that you return to again and again. When things feel really rough, it's important to remember why you might have committed to sharing your life with another person to begin with. And every now and again, it helps to remind each other of the bumps in the road that you've traveled together.

We're Only Human

THERE'S A CONCEPT known as *Lashon Hara*, which translates literally to "Bad Tongue," meaning speaking ill of others: not quite gossip, nearly slander, and nothing nice. To take it one step further, not only are you not supposed to speak ill of others, you aren't supposed to say bad things about yourself either. In Psalm 106, the psalmist recounts many of the low points his people have experienced over the generations. In Verse 6, he also says:

> We have sinned with our fathers, we have done iniquitously, we have dealt wickedly.

In theory, he is speaking *Lashon Hara* about himself and his nation. It feels more like humbleness, though. It's comforting to know that even the greatest among us have fallen or made mistakes or done the things we've sworn we never would.

Let It All Out

ONE OF THE BEST and worst elements of prayer is the ability to pour out one's heart and emotions to a blank canvas. Everyone's relationship with his or her God is unique and completely individual. You get to picture or imagine what your particular deity is like and you know the comfort of your relationship with him or her. But the thing is, unlike face-to-face relationships, you don't always get a reaction, much less the response to your prayers that you might hope for, and sometimes the answer is simply, "No." In Psalm 44:24 King David feels abandoned and says to God:

> *Awake, why sleepest Thou, oh Lord?*
> *Arouse Thyself, forsake not forever.*

While prayer can help you to sort through your feelings, sometimes you just want to cry out and beg not to be abandoned. And sometimes, much as you hope for a better resolution, the answer is simply, "No."

Merciful Beyond Measure

IT SOMETIMES FEELS like a full-time job to try to become a better person. And despite my best efforts to remain calm and even-tempered during times of great stress, I notice myself growing annoyed with some people while I might have endless amounts of patience for others. I try to analyze my reactions and I spend time wondering what makes me more compassionate with some people and regularly and repeatedly annoyed with others. In Psalm 108:5 the psalmist says:

> *For Thy mercy is great above the heavens,*
> *and Thy truth reacheth unto the skies.*

Much as I wish that I had endless reserves of patience and mercy, I'm only human. But I am trying. And some days, that's the best I can do.

Harsh and Indirect

B EING A GOOD PERSON and standing up for yourself are not mutually exclusive. And being a person who believes in the power of prayer doesn't mean that you have to accept mistreatment or abuse from others. In addition to love, honor, and praise, many of the themes of ancient prayers include outright discussions of vengeance. Psalm 109 is pretty harsh; in Verse 9, the psalmist says of his enemies:

> *Let his children be fatherless,*
> *and his wife a widow.*

This is not a direct curse or bad wish, but rather a more elegant way of truly cursing someone. Because let's face it, sometimes we really do need to let out our frustrations. My mother never wishes ill on those who have treated her badly, but she frequently has a wicked glint in her eye when she recites this particular Psalm.

Rise Above

I HAD A REALLY INTERESTING conversation today with a brand-new friend. We compared notes about our best moments as well as some of the crummier turns that each of our lives had taken and how, for the most part, we'd been battered and bruised but were still doing fine—in some ways, even better than before. In Psalm 110:2, the psalmist says:

Rule thou in the midst of thine enemies.

I read this Psalm through so many times before this line jumped out at me. And suddenly it was so clear to me. Life throws a lot at you and some of the time you're surrounded by bad people or bad circumstances. It isn't much of a challenge to be in charge of your life when everything is going your way. It is, however, no small miracle to keep going and learn how to thrive when things get really tough.

What's Your Legacy?

WE ALL HAVE GREAT HOPES for our lives. Some include the basics, including health and prosperity and love. Some are smaller in scale but can feel so urgent, like keeping fit or learning a new skill. One of the benefits of prayer is giving people a big-picture approach to things. When you compare thousands of years of history, including calamities and victories, and compare them to our own day-to-day struggles, it can all feel daunting to try to create a history as rich as that of those that came before us. In Psalm 111:7, the psalmist says:

The works of His hands are truth and justice;
all His precepts are sure.

Sometimes the most impressive legacies are the most fundamental. Remaining true to yourself and your beliefs can be an incredibly empowering legacy.

Muse and Inspiration

WHILE PSALMS CAN HELP serve as daily inspiration and lessons for life, they've proven to be inspirational to poets and composers as well. Psalm 112 is one of two Psalms (along with 111) composed as an acrostic puzzle of sorts, with each few words or couplets starting with the Aleph Bet, the Hebrew alphabet. As "Beatus Vir," the Latin for "Happy is the man," the first few words of the Psalm, it has provided musical inspiration for composers including Monteverdi, Vivaldi, and Mozart. If you sometimes feel tapped out and can't make yourself pray or can't find meaning in the words, try to envision them through the eyes of a poet or artist. Perhaps another level of inspiration will bring a different kind of meaning back to you.

A Mother's Prayer

THERE ARE MANY INSTANCES of overlap in prayer themes and wording. Psalm 113 has a similar composition to Hannah's Prayer, offered when she had finally given birth to the prophet Samuel. There are several women in the Old Testament whose yearning and prayers for children permeate their stories. Sarah was childless for decades before finally giving birth to Isaac at the age of 90. It's said that the reason that God waited so long to give a child to Sarah was because he loved hearing her prayers and didn't want them to stop. Psalm 113:9 says:

Who maketh the barren woman to dwell in
her house as a joyful mother of children.

This Psalm can serve as comfort for those still hoping to experience that particular joy.

Things That Make You Smile

P SALM 114 IS ONE of the six Psalms included in the *Hallel* or "Praise" prayer said on special holidays. Different parts of the prayers are set to different tunes, nearly all of them upbeat. Every time I read Verse 4, which discusses the joy felt when the Israelites were freed from slavery in Egypt, I have to smile:

> *The mountains skipped like rams,*
> *the hills like young sheep.*

There are many holiday traditions that are geared to children, to keep them involved and engaged in the preparations and ritual. Prayers like this one can bring out the kid in adults, presenting fun, happy images and connotations to prayer, instead of the heavier liturgy.

Materialism

IN *WALDEN*, HENRY DAVID THOREAU wrote about his years spent at his cabin on Walden Pond and his quest for a simpler life. Thoreau didn't have as much as a carpet because then he'd require a carpet beater and then a hook to hang the carpet beater, and so on until his own life would be bogged down by possessions. In Psalm 115:4 the psalmist says:

> *Their idols are silver and gold,*
> *the work of men's hands.*

We all know people like that, people who worship money and all that it can buy. There's a Hebrew expression, *Marbeh nichasim, marbeh da'agot,* which loosely translates to "The more possessions you have, the more worries you have." We all like our creature comforts and luxuries, but when the things you own start to own you, it's time to take a step back and have a good look at the truly important things in life.

Not All Men

POPULAR FICTION, angry break-up songs, and women's magazine articles would have you believe that all men are universally awful. They'll hurt you and cheat on you and break your heart for sport. And once your heart is damaged beyond repair, these no-good men will stomp on it again for good measure. Only that's not the case, is it? Both men and women are more complicated than clichés would indicate. In Psalm 116:11 the psalmist says:

> *I said in my haste; All men are liars.*

But all men aren't liars, are they? And having bad experiences or heartache doesn't mean that you're doomed to more of the same. I think of the men who have stomped on my heart either intentionally or for sport, and I still don't blame every man. And I think of the men in my life, who are loving and loyal and honest and imperfect, and I completely agree with this Psalm.

Brevity

WITH ONLY 16 WORDS and two verses, Psalm 117 is the shortest of the 150 Psalms. In Verse 2, the psalmist says:

For His kindness has overwhelmed us.

Well, not to be petty, but wouldn't you think that someone overwhelmed by the kindness of others would be unable to contain his or her enthusiasm? And that they'd express said zeal and gratitude with verses filled with sparkling details and endless attention to detail? It was Shakespeare who said in *Hamlet*, "Brevity is the soul of wit." Though I tend to be an effusive person, even I can recognize the fact that sometimes a very well placed word or two packs more of an emotional punch than tomes full of empty words.

Every Day, a Good Day

I SOMETIMES JOKE that I like weather too much to live someplace where the weather is perfect all the time. I thrive on contrast and like cloudy days because they allow me time to catch my breath and not feel so "on" all the time. I sometimes like cold days because I need the crisp weather for clarity or contrast. And much as I complain about the slushy gray snow that we have in New York City, I revel in the hour or two when the snow first falls and the world is blanketed and pure for mere moments. Psalm 118:24 says:

> *This is the day which the Lord hath made;*
> *we will rejoice and be glad in it.*

We all have very terrible "no good very bad" days, as Judith Viorst wrote, but we all have very good ones as well. The main thing to remember is that every day has the potential to be better than the one that came before.

Knowledge Is Power

WITH A TOTAL OF 176 verses, Psalm 119 is the longest of the 150 Psalms. It's also the longest chapter in the Bible—even longer than entire books of both the Old and New Testament. This Psalm includes alphabetic acrostic puzzles and other word wizardry. Verses 98 and 99 both refer to learning, and are worth noting:

> *Thy commandments make me wiser than*
> *mine enemies: for they are ever with me.*
> *And I have more understanding*
> *than all my teachers.*

The second line, from Verse 99, is also often translated as "I have learned or gained knowledge from all of my teachers." Whether these lines refer to learning how to live a structured life by following the most basic commandments, or being able to find even a grain of knowledge from anyone willing to teach you, wisdom strengthens you.

Fight for Peace

THERE ARE SO MANY ISSUES of great controversy in our society that it can sometimes feel
nearly impossible to speak one's mind freely in
an ostensibly free country. Longtime friends fall
out over their political beliefs, while coworkers all
but snarl at each other when discussing military
maneuvers. Perhaps I'm oversimplifying the matter, but I don't think that anyone is ever excited
about the idea of war or the potential aftermath.
I do think, though, that there are principles both
political and personal that are well worth fighting
for, though many of us are tired of fighting. In
Psalm 120:7 the psalmist says:

> *I am all peace; but when I speak,*
> *they are for war.*

Sometimes you may have the best intentions and
hope not to engage with a potential enemy, but if
they push too hard the only thing possible to protect yourself, is to push right back.

Raise Your Expectations

PSALM 121 BEGINS with one of the more familiar and popular verses, when the psalmist says:

I will lift up mine eyes unto the mountains:
from whence shall my help come?

In the next verse, he answers his own questions:

My help cometh from the Lord,
who made heaven and earth.

It's almost a reflex for people to raise their eyes heavenward when seeking some sort of salvation. This Psalm suggests that we shouldn't be scanning the horizons for help, when help is found with the one who created everything we see. To take it a step further, in Verse 4, the psalmist says that his God "doth neither slumber nor sleep." It's the ultimate reassurance. Not only is God his salvation, but also one who isn't tied to the laws or rules of mankind.

Home Peaceful Home

IN EXPLORING PSALM 122, I read a lot of accompanying commentary about the qualities of the home that is repeatedly referred to within the texts. And, of course, it's possible that the hopes and wishes and physical manifestations mentioned are all hypothetical and metaphor. But sometimes it's most inspiring to imagine that the words of joy and hope are just that—inspirational words for the here and now. At the end of Verse 6 and the beginning of Verse 7, the psalmist says:

> *May those who love you be secure.*
> *May there be peace within your walls.*

I think that's become my favorite new wish. And I love that sentiment so much I might just embroider it on a pillow.

Don't Give Up

ALTHOUGH I'M NOT a timid sort, I often wonder just how persistent to be about things. If someone doesn't answer an email I've sent for a day or so (or an hour if I'm really anxious), does it mean that they hate me, or that they're just really, really busy? And if it's easy to become insecure when trying to communicate with people, how much more frustrating is it to try to communicate with God? In Psalm 123 at the end of Verse 2, the psalmist speaks of several types of interpersonal relationships that compare to his relationship to his God, and then says:

Our eyes look unto the Lord our God,
until He has mercy on us.

It feels like a wonderful lesson in hope, faith, and persistence.

Don't Magnify Your Problems

I AM A WORRIER by nature. I worry about the obvious things, like the health and happiness of my loved ones. I worry about external threats. I worry about keeping clients happy. In a given day I'd say that sometimes I just sit around and worry about the fact that I worry too much. Because worrying is such an incredibly useless emotion. It doesn't actively change anything, and it certainly doesn't affect the outcome of a situation—for better or worse. In Psalm 124:3 when the psalmist speaks of his enemies he says:

> *Then they had swallowed us up alive,*
> *when their wrath was kindled against us.*

He had good reason to worry, he was facing life or death situations. But for the rest of us, worrying can just drain any of the joy.

Play Fair

I T WOULD SEEM PRETTY OBVIOUS that people who are good and just should be treated well and have the best things in life, right? Well, that's a nice theory, but it's not always the way that life plays out. Sometimes the most wonderful human beings have the hardest times in life. And it can make the rest of us despair for any level of fairness or justice in the universe. In Psalm 125:4, the psalmist says:

> *Do good, oh Lord, unto the good, and to them that are upright in their hearts.*

It's a gentle plea to God to remember to care for those who deserve it most. And it's a good lesson for the rest of us. It shouldn't always be the squeaky wheel that gets the grease, but rather the one that is most deserving.

Hard Work and Perspective

ISN'T IT AMAZING how you can have one specific thought or meaning in your mind for years, and then reread something and suddenly gain clarity? For years, every time that I read Psalm 126:5, I thought it meant that you have to go through misery to ever hope for happiness:

> They that sow in tears shall reap in joy.

As I edge ever closer to sustained happiness in my life, I realize that suffering doesn't have to be part of that particular equation. Instead, I'd like to think this verse means that you have to invest yourself, your time, and your best efforts in your family, career, art, or hobby. The harder you work, the more you'll produce.

Sharp Blessings

CHILDREN ARE AMONG the greatest blessings in life. And yet the composer of this Psalm, King David, didn't always have the easiest time with his own offspring. Absalom revolted against his father, and some commentators say that in this particular Psalm, King David had to deal with the reality that it was his son Solomon and not he who would build the temple. In Verses 127: 4-5 David says:

> *As arrows in the hand of a mighty man,*
> *so are the children of one's youth. Happy*
> *is the man that hath his quiver full of them.*

It's an interesting metaphor for a father to use, comparing children to the sharpness of an arrow and the happiness of being a youthful father, before disagreements and strife can set in. Being a parent isn't always easy, but David seemed to be able to balance his joy in fatherhood along with his pain.

Onward and Upward

SOME OF THE GREATEST success stories involve people with incredibly humble beginnings going through dramatic changes to reinvent themselves and overcome the past. These stories are uplifting in great part because the people triumphed over difficult circumstances not only to rise above, but also to soar. In Psalm 129:2 the psalmist says:

Much have they afflicted me from my youth up; but they have not prevailed against me.

Even some of the greatest historical figures come from less than stellar beginnings. Perhaps they were bullied or tormented by their peers. Or their family life was volatile. Perhaps your own childhood or teen years or even young adulthood wasn't the stuff of dreams. But circumstances change and so do people. And if you can rise above a rocky past, there's no limit to what you can accomplish in the future.

Turn Sorrow into Inspiration

DID YOU EVER NOTICE that when you're in a bad mood you try endlessly to figure out the cause, but when you're in a good mood you just kind of go with it? I know that I'm guilty of just that. I'll endlessly try to figure out what causes my blue moods instead of simply accepting that, like the weather, moods are rapidly changeable. Psalm 130 is one of the most famous and most truly sorrowful of all Psalms. It begins:

> *A Song of Ascents. Out of the depths have*
> *I called Thee Oh Lord.*

This psalmist is not alone in turning misery into inspiration. A long list of composers, including Bach, Liszt, Handel, Mendelssohn, and Mozart all set portions of this Psalm to music. So the next time you've got a bad case of the blues, take encouragement from the others who came before and transformed personal pain to triumph.

Balanced Bragging

I N THIS LIFE, it's important to take credit for your accomplishments and best moments. More than that, sometimes it's crucial to brag about them. Because who are we kidding? Unless you hire your own personal PR rep, no one will talk about your greatest successes unless you do. And we all know how frustrating it is when others take credit for our hard work. Then again, with social media in overdrive, it feels like all anyone does these days is engage in promoting themselves and every minute detail of their lives. In Psalm 131:1, the psalmist says:

My heart is not haughty, nor mine eyes lofty.

And yet in other Psalms he does in fact discuss all of his great triumphs in great detail. Perhaps the lesson here is to balance your bragging with true modesty and not the dreaded and completely insincere "humblebrag."

Take Time Off from Worrying

WE TEND TO THINK of ourselves as an enlightened culture. Sensitivity in both sexes is a desired ideal; even our leaders tear up when discussing great tragedies. And in going through the ancient texts, it becomes clear that the kings and rulers admitted their own vulnerabilities repeatedly. The psalmist is so worried about having to make major nations on behalf of his people—so much so, that he barely allows himself sleep. In Psalm 132:4 he says:

> *I will not give sleep to mine eyes,*
> *nor slumber to mine eyelids.*

We've all had nights so bad that we've barely slept, because we were so troubled by the previous day's occurrences or panicked about the day ahead. But everything seems scarier and more intense at night. So maybe it really is good advice to set aside some time every day for worrying and leave nighttime for sleep and rejuvenation.

Reconciliation

WHEN I STARTED WRITING this book people kept telling me their favorite Psalms and urged me to include them. And at one point or another, nearly every Psalm was mentioned, with many coming up time and time again. Because Psalms are included in so many different prayers, many of them appear in daily or holiday prayers. Psalm 133 is one of the most universally familiar ones, Verse 3 in particular:

> *Behold, how good and how pleasant it is*
> *for brethren to dwell together in unity.*

On a personal level, family strife can sour almost all aspects of life: bickering siblings, competitive sisters, or brothers who refuse to help care for elderly parents—it all feels familiar. But sometimes the best way to win a family argument is to be the first to stop fighting.

In the Wee Hours

WHAT IS IT about the nighttime that seems to magnify all problems? I wish there was a magic formula to make those after-dark panic attacks dissipate if not disappear entirely. In Psalm 134 the psalmist seems to have an alternative to fretting the night away. The Psalm begins:

> Behold, bless the Lord, all servants of
> the Lord who stand in the house of
> the Lord at night.

Rabbi David Kimhi, a medieval rabbi from Provence also known by the acronym the "Radak," commented prodigiously on the Book of Psalms. He says this verse refers to the pious souls who get up in middle of the night to pray or learn good things. While I'm not suggesting setting an alarm clock for the wee hours to catch up on prayer, it might be a nice option to catch up on your meditations or prayers during those dark hours when sleep eludes you.

The Signs Are Everywhere

P EOPLE ARE CONSTANTLY searching for meaning in their lives. And sometimes they'll latch onto coincidence or superstition when true meaning seems elusive. That pursuit of meaning can lead people in directions that might take them down instead of building them up. In Psalm 135:9, in discussing the Israelites' exodus from Egypt, the psalmist says:

> *He sent signs and wonders*
> *into the midst of thee.*

It's said that in ancient times miracles were visible to all. In our own times though, things seem murkier or harder to relate to. But if you open your eyes to even the most basic daily occurrences, you might just be dazzled by what you have been taking for granted. We have seen miraculous advances in medicine, tech, and travel with new discoveries emerging daily.

Many Mercies

As with many of the Psalms, Psalm 136 is included in the liturgy of numerous faiths and religions, and repeated in the prayers of numerous holidays and festivals. The psalmist lists many of the qualities and mercies of God, and in Verse 25 says:

Who giveth food to all flesh.

This highlights the generosity of providing sustenance on such a global scale. The Talmud teaches us that the lesson we're meant to glean from this is that, if God can take time to create great stores of food throughout the world and in every nation, who are we to ignore the plight of our starving brethren? Many of us admire the generosity of philanthropists who change the world on a global scale. But you can change your own world by buying a hungry person a sandwich or volunteering at a soup kitchen.

Whatever Gets You Through

IT'S HARD TO PINPOINT one Psalm as being more widely recognized than another. But Psalm 137 may be one of the best known. It begins with the line:

> *By the rivers of Babylon, there we sat down,*
> *yea, we wept, when we remembered Zion.*

This Psalm contains universal themes that have inspired classical, pop and even reggae music. The leitmotifs of the Psalm include the abject despair of a nation forced out of its home and into exile; remembrances of the joys of a better time; avowals never to forget the joy that once was, and declarations of future vengeance. We've all gone through times of personal turmoil that have made us feel like we've been exiled from our day-to-day lives and any sense of normalcy. And in trying to get through, we've likely experienced a range of emotions that might have shocked or appalled our ordinary selves. But life isn't always predictable, and neither are our reactions to the curveballs we're sometimes thrown.

Say It Like You Mean It

BESIDES A VAST SPECTRUM of emotions ranging from loneliness to neediness to fear and rage expressed throughout the Psalms, there's an underlying and consistent theme of praise and thanks. Yet the beginning of Psalm 138 made me take another look at all of the others. It begins:

I will give Thee thanks with my whole heart.

Is it possible that rest of the Psalms were less sincere than this one? Doubtful, but it's all too easy to offer insincere platitudes—easier yet to toss off a halfhearted thank you if we think much effort wasn't expended on the part of someone who helped us out. But it's crucial never to take for granted the generosity of spirit or generosity of giving. After all, someone who's been generous to you could be helping someone else out, but they've chosen to help you instead.

With Some Help from Your Friends

DESPITE MYRIAD INSECURITIES instilled in me and magnified by our hypercritical society, I've always been a fairly confident person. As the child of immigrants, I straddled the worlds of the old and the new and never quite fit in anywhere, which is why I had to find my own way most of the time—and still do. In Psalm 139, the psalmist discusses his relationship with his God and being unable to hide either his emotions or physical self, even if he chose to. In Verse 17 he says:

> *And to me, how dear are your friends,*
> *Oh Lord! How great is their sum!*

Sometimes society can make us feel like misfits if we feel too deeply or strongly about something unpopular or considered passé. But faith doesn't ever go out of style. And finding others who share your beliefs can make the journey a joy instead of a challenge.

Sharpen Your Best Traits

Aᴄᴄᴏʀᴅɪɴɢ ᴛᴏ ꜰᴀᴍɪʟʏ ʟᴇɢᴇɴᴅ, when my much-adored cousin Cookie became engaged to my cousin Saul, a meddlesome friend approached her and warned her against marrying into my family. Cookie was told that my mother's family was known for their sharp way of speaking and that apparently their tongues were "sharper than the mohel's knife." (The mohel is the person who performs the circumcision ceremony on an 8-day-old baby boy.) That's pretty sharp indeed. In Psalm 140:4, in speaking of his enemies, the psalmist says:

> *They have sharpened their tongue*
> *like a serpent.*

And while David suffered mightily at the hands of his enemies, having a sharp tongue isn't always the worst thing—provided that you know when to use it. Look at the cutting wisdom of Oscar Wilde and Dorothy Parker, both of whom used their wit as their greatest weapons. Which of your own greatest faults can you turn into a valued asset?

Thoughts on Criticism

I N PSALM 141, King David asks God for help with being a better person. He asks for help in guarding his tongue and in avoiding temptations. In Verse 5 he says:

> *Let the righteous smite me in kindness,*
> *and let them correct me.*

While David is asking for help in accepting criticism, it also feels like a lesson in giving criticism as well. Before attempting to rebuke or correct anyone, consider your own motives and intent. Are you actually trying to help them, or does their way of doing things just get on your nerves? Conversely, how good are you at accepting criticism? Are you open to negative feedback, or do you tune out as soon as someone says something you don't like?

Release Useless Emotions

M Y CATHOLIC FRIENDS believe they possess the greatest level of guilt known to mankind, while my Jewish friends insist that guilt is their birthright. Then there are my friends who believe their mothers, priests, or schoolteachers exclusively have instilled in them a lifelong level of guilt unmatched by others. For the past few years I've been trying to learn how to release useless emotions from my life, and guilt and regret top my list. In Psalm 142:8, the psalmist says:

Bring my soul out of prison.

To me, a soul imprisoned is usually that way due to the overwhelming and overpowering emotions brought on by guilt. If you're reading a book about reclaiming and channeling your faith, I know something about you already: You are a good person trying to find ways to be even better. And unless you learn from past mistakes, you're imprisoning your soul and not allowing yourself to move forward. So let go of the guilt, release the regret and learn to move forward to a better future.

Speak Up

I F YOU'RE FORTUNATE, every day is an opportunity to learn something new. And if you're even luckier, you learned useful lessons at a young age and have moved on and honed your skills over the years. And maybe you've even shared your lessons with others. We are not born knowing how to defend ourselves. And so some of us are bullied and some are taken advantage of, and like the Little Mermaid of the Hans Christian Andersen fairy tale, some of us trade our voices or power to speak up or defend ourselves for the opportunity to be loved. But no one should have to give up the right to speak for themselves. Psalm 44 starts off by saying:

> *Blessed be the Lord my rock, who traineth*
> *my hands for war, and my fingers for battle.*

If you've never learned how to defend yourself and your best interests, it's never too late to learn.

Everything in Its Time

HAVE YOU BEEN FOLLOWING the movement toward eating locally grown and produced foods? So-called "locavores" prefer sustainable food sources and would rather not have their food travel long distances before ending up on their plates. Technically this isn't a modern trend but rather a move to reclaim a healthier lifestyle and way of appreciating food. In Psalm 145:15 the psalmist says:

Thou givest them their food in due season.

On the surface this line shows appreciation for a God who provides food as needed, which in itself is no small thing. But to take it deeper, it's also the notion of sustenance and being given the things we need to survive when they're most needed. What sustains you most in life?

Stay True to Yourself

DESPITE YOUR BEST EFFORTS at trying to lead a certain kind of life, external influences can creep in. And with so many external enticements clamoring for your attention, one of the hardest things in life is staying true to yourself. After all, popular culture wants you to want to be just like everyone else. Advertisers need you to be dissatisfied with what you have, and always wanting the next shiny thing. In Psalm 146:6, the psalmist refers to God as he:

Who keepeth truth forever.

This means, not merely staying true to an ideal for as long as it's trendy or convenient, but being in it for the long haul. We've all gone through different phases in our lives and then transitioned to the next with barely a backward glance. But trying to keep true to timeless ideals can be a lifelong pursuit without any obvious rewards other than believing in yourself and what you know in your heart to be right.

A Greater Love

WHO HASN'T SUFFERED the agony of a broken heart? I hate even thinking about all those nights spent sobbing or listening to old love songs or immersed in self-doubt, wondering how things could or should have been different. And despite everyone saying that time would heal the pain, the residual pang would still stab your heart every now and again until that day when you wake up and realize that everything doesn't hurt quite as much as it once did. And then another day, you just feel fine. In Psalm 147:3, the psalmist refers to God as he:

Who healeth the broken in heart

I don't think anyone takes that literally, but perhaps it's more than simply poetic verse. Sometimes having a deep and abiding belief in something larger than yourself can lift you up out of your own misery. And continuing to love your God, even when romantic love has failed you, might be the cure for what ails a broken heart.

Praise and Protect

THOUGH IN THEORY I can understand the majority of the words in the Psalms, sometimes I don't quite understand the way that they flow together. I suppose it's somewhat comparable to the Old English used in *Beowulf* or Chaucer's *Canterbury Tales*; at times, the modern usage doesn't match up to the more ancient texts. In Psalm 149:6, the psalmist says in speaking of the righteous:

> *Let the high praises of God be in their mouth,*
> *and a two-edged sword in their hand.*

Let them be pious and sing praise, but also protect themselves and fight their enemies. This feels like a pretty timeless sentiment. It's important to hold onto your faith, but it's just as crucial to be aware of the potential dangers in the world around you.

A Final Thought

THE FINAL WORDS in any great work of literature have to be momentous and hopefully as great as the work itself. Those last words have to sustain the reader and leave him or her with the full weight of the entire book. And the final words in Psalm 150, the final Psalm, are:

> *Let every thing that hath breath*
> *praise the Lord. Hallelujah!*

It feels like such an upbeat way of closing the cycle of Psalms. The Book of Psalms covers fear and bravery, loss and love, war and peace and overall devotion, gratitude and deep love for a greater power. And the nature of the Book of Psalms is that as soon as you're done reading, be it on a daily, weekly, or monthly basis, you start all over again. It's a wonderful way to end a book that's all about need balanced with gratitude. If you breathe, you should be grateful to the one that made you.

The Power of
the Spoken Word

THERE'S A SOMEWHAT SHORT prayer in the daily services that is called by, and begins with, the words *Baruch She'Amar*, which means:

Blessed is the one who spoke.

The next few words refer to the creation of the world. Common understanding is that those words refer to God, who spoke his desires and thereby created the world. In thinking about ancient prayer in general, it's interesting to reflect on how the most gorgeous prayers are lyrical on paper, but can move one to tears when sung by a congregation. In this case, perhaps the blessing is also on those who speak the words aloud and give them the power of the group. Though it's wonderful to read through prayers to yourself, every now and again, it's great to channel the power of the group and raise your voices in unison.

Tefillin the Blanks

I F YOU'VE EVER SEEN an observant Jew swaying while wearing a pair of small black boxes affixed to his head and arm, you've seen him *davening* (praying) while wearing tefillin, or phylacteries, from the Greek word for "protect." Tefillin are small leather boxes containing scrolls with portions of the Torah (the first five books of the Hebrew scriptures). I thought I should mention this because, in reading the prayer said before wearing the tefillin, I was struck by the language:

It is a sign upon your arm.

This made me think of wedding or engagement rings, which upon immediate glance exhibit to the world the wearer's marital status. What looks odd to some, might just be a form of commitment to another—be it religious or romantic.

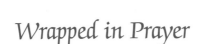

Wrapped in Prayer

SOME YEARS BACK I managed a Judaica store on the Upper West Side of Manhattan. Two things surprised me most about our clientele: The first was the collection of traditionally observant and incredibly down-to-earth celebrities who regularly stopped in to buy their ritual objects and gifts for the holidays (a seder plate for the Spielbergs!). The second big eye opener was the fact that prayer shawls were less about representing a specific religion, sex, or age group than they were a highly symbolic, almost universally popular item for both sexes and people of all faiths. There's a prayer said for putting on the Tallit or prayer shawl that includes the words:

> *Donning light as a garment,*
> *the heavens stretching out as a curtain.*

It's such a beautiful way of describing a garment that for all intents and purposes wraps a person in a realm of spirituality and personal conviction.

(Doing) More Is Better

THERE'S A PRAYER CALLED *Eilu Devarim*, or "These Things (are without limit)" that lists 10 of the things we should give of ourselves or do without measure. Some are no-brainers like honoring your parents, but they also cover essentials that we might not have thought of on our own—rejoicing with a bride and groom for instance. We all lead such crazy, busy lives that it's hard to keep track of who should be calling whom. But maybe that's the best lesson of all: stop keeping track and give freely of yourself, your time, and your love to those who matter most. Wouldn't it be amazing if we could start a global initiative not only to stop keeping track of favors done, but also to try to do more for others first?

If you've ever vowed to do more for others, this list might provide some inspiration and ideas of how to start and what to do:

> *These are the obligations without measure,*
> *whose reward, too, is without measure:*
>
> *to honor father and mother;*
>
> *to perform acts of love and kindness;*
>
> *to attend the house of study daily;*

to welcome the stranger;

to visit the sick;

to rejoice with bride and groom;

to console the bereaved;

to pray with sincerity;

to make peace when there is strife.

And the study of Torah is equal to them all-

because it leads to them all.

Satisfied

ONE OF THE MORE BAFFLING dichotomies of modern life is the fact that, the more we have or have access to, the more dissatisfied we feel with the things we still don't have. Who hasn't felt that aching void at some point or another? And while it can be distracting and lots of fun to indulge in some satisfying retail therapy every now and again, the new and shiny doesn't provide more than a temporary Band-Aid or quick mood fix. Psalm 107:9 says:

For He hath satisfied the longing soul, and
the hungry soul He hath filled with good.

Sometimes you have to open yourself up and acknowledge the void before you can fill it. And sometimes being dissatisfied can be the contrast that you need to help you to recognize true satisfaction.

Count Your Blessings

THERE ARE A LOT of playful songs, prayers, and melodies sung on Passover that have very serious themes; *Dayenu* or "Enough/It Would Have Been Enough" is one of them. The complete song first appeared in medieval times in the Haggadah, the specific prayer book used on Passover, and counts the many blessings experienced by the ancient Israelites on their journey out of slavery in Egypt. There's one line that to me elevates the ways in which we not only count our own blessings, but also are inspired to help others:

> *If He had split the sea but had not us*
> *pass through on dry land, it would*
> *have been enough.*

When we realize how fortunate we are in our own lives, it's easier to try to help others with their own. And while it's a great thing to help pull someone out of a bad place, trying to help them find the clear path ahead to better times is an even greater act of generosity.

Find Your Way Back

*E*ITZ *CHAYIM HE*, or "She Is the Tree of Life," is a song sung on the Sabbath and when returning the Torah scrolls to the ark. The tree of life in question is the Torah, or the first five books of the ancient Hebrew Bible, the study of which is said to be life-giving or life-extending. The term originates in Genesis and is used several times in Proverbs. I love this line:

> *Cause us to learn, renew and return,*
> *Just as in days of old.*

I believe that this illustrates an acceptance of those who have fallen away from their faith or practice, and are unsure of how to return or if it's even possible to do so. It's a realization that we can't always be the people we hope to be, and a gentle plea for God to help us find our way back when we've lost our way.

Instruments of Joy

D ID YOU EVER HEAR a piece of music that was so incredibly beautiful that it touched your soul and moved you to tears? Maybe it was a solo violin concerto, or perhaps it was a rock guitarist so in tune with his instrument that he elevated the sound to pure emotion. I'm not of the mind that there is only one way to express your faith or belief. So while prayer can help to focus or ground you, sometimes you move past the words and find faith in unexpected places. In Psalm 98:6, the psalmist says:

> *With trumpets and sound of the horn*
> *shout ye before the king, the Lord.*

Sometimes a baby banging a fork on her high chair tray can represent the pure joy and emotion that a thousand poets seem to miss.

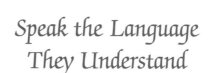

Speak the Language They Understand

AS A KID, I had a hard time with authority and questioned things I was told to believe without question. I remember a conversation with my elementary school principal, who said something rather sarcastic about "the illustrious Rachel Weingarten." Though I had a pretty sophisticated vocabulary for a fifth grader, I had no idea of what "illustrious" meant and told my principal it was unfair of him to deliberately use words I could not understand. In Psalm 99:7 the psalmist says:

He spoke unto them in the pillar of cloud.

It's said the countenance of God is so fearsome and incomprehensible that he'd appear to his prophets in guises they could comprehend—a pillar of smoke in this case, a burning bush for Moses. If you truly want to connect with someone, don't talk down to them or use words or concepts that elude them. Prayer offers a universal language of connectivity, something many of us could use more of in our daily lives.

It Isn't Old-Fashioned
to Have Faith

A S A PERSON OF FAITH, there's a good chance that you've probably had awkward moments over the years where you've had to explain your beliefs to other people. They might have smiled politely, but chances are good that they wondered at how someone so seemingly in touch with the outside world could hold onto such seemingly old-fashioned beliefs. But what's old-fashioned about wanting to keep believing in something instead of choosing to believe in a random and frequently cruel universe? In Psalm 100:5 says:

For the Lord is good;
His mercy endureth forever;
and His faithfulness unto all generations.

It's wonderful to think that it's not only that you believe in God and follow the beliefs of your ancestors, but that you are putting your faith in a God who returns that faithfulness for generations.

Bad Influences

You'd be surprised how many prayers ask God to keep an eye on his people (and in particular, on the person doing the praying) and to protect them from unexpected external situations. In the morning prayers, there's one that's mostly an appeal. It begins *Yehi Ratzon*:

May it be the Will,

It then goes through a list of requests to be saved from bad influences of every variety. One line includes these two: "bad friends and bad neighbors." It was unexpected to realize that the ancient texts included "frenemies," or friends that aren't really all that friendly. I think that sometimes reading and acknowledging certain words, or if there's time, saying them aloud can be empowering as well. So listen up, faux friends and annoying neighbors: You've officially been given notice. From this moment forward, I really do intend to surround myself with people who help make my days and life better. Who's with me?

Power of the Spoken Word

T HERE'S A SOMEWHAT SHORT prayer in the daily services that is called, and begins with the words, *Baruch She'Amar*:

> *Blessed is the One who spoke.*

The next few words refer to the creation of the world. Common understanding is that those words refer to God, who spoke his desires and thereby created the world. In thinking about ancient prayer in general, it's interesting to reflect on how even the most simple prayers can move one to tears when sung by a congregation. In this case, perhaps the blessing is also on those who speak the words aloud and give them the power of the group. So, though it's wonderful to read prayers to yourself, every now and again, it's great to channel the power of the group and raise your voices in unison.

The Good Old Days

IN THE MIDST of the morning prayers there's a segment called "Master of Legions," that begins by asking that God answer these prayers soon. It also requests that he remember his people fondly, and includes quotes from Malachi 3:4 asking that God accept the prayers of his people:

As in days gone by, as in former years.

When relationships are new, it's easy to want to keep your beloved happy. But as time goes on, people take each other for granted and seem less inclined to work as hard to put each other's needs before their own. The next time you get annoyed by the needs of someone close to you, try to remember how you might have responded to their requests or needs when your relationship was still brand-new.

It Goes Both Ways

WHEN TIMES ARE DIFFICULT it can feel as though you're speaking into a vacuum instead of having your heartfelt prayers connect to your God. Until I really started delving into the ancient prayers, I never quite realized this additional step existed formally, but a recurring theme was the composer of the prayers respectfully explaining to God that they wanted their prayers acknowledged and answered. In other words, you don't just barge in making demands, but you must explain your needs. In Chronicles 2:6, Solomon says:

> Yet, Lord, my God, give attention to Your
> servant's prayer and his plea for mercy.
> Hear the cry and the prayer that Your
> servant is praying in Your presence.

It's probably a great game plan in life as well. Don't barge into someone's office or even their inbox making demands; prepare them first for what you might be asking, and you'll probably have a better chance of being answered.

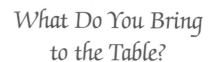

What Do You Bring to the Table?

A S WITH MANY TOPICS dealing with faith, there is much about ancient prayer that can seem dated, if not completely irrelevant. And it doesn't make you a nonbeliever to have those thoughts; it means you are trying to incorporate ancient practices and ideals into your modern existence. One really touchy topic is that of offering a sacrifice of sorts. To put things into historical perspective, animal sacrifice was a way of worship for nearly every ancient culture and faith. The good news is that it's been substituted with fervent prayers and holidays. A much better option all around, wouldn't you agree? One prayer begins with these words:

And God spoke to Moses.

There's also a line in this prayer about offerings of bread (food) and incense. It isn't a bribe to try to offer small gifts to those in a position of power or just to be thoughtful. Don't just ask for things; try to offer as well.

Respect All

ONE OF THE GREATEST LESSONS I've learned from my parents is to respect everyone equally. True respect, and not just a cursory level of deference. Of course, there's an extra layer afforded to people in a particular position of importance, but we were taught never to discriminate based on any sort of religious, cultural, racial or socioeconomic basis. Chronicles 2, 6:19 says:

> *Yet have thou respect unto the prayer of thy servant, and to his supplication.*

That line feels multilayered because the person praying has denigrated his position to that of a servant, yet he is still asking for respect in having his prayers heard. I'm a firm believer in treating people with the respect you hope to receive from others. It feels like common sense, but some people seem to lack the sense to treat people as anything but common.

Prayer: A Direct Line

WHEN WE'RE VERY YOUNG, we seem to believe that we can talk to anyone and everyone; not only that, we expect them to answer. And it takes a lot of living and a lot of ups and downs to make us realize that things don't quite work that way. As adults, we might be frustrated by some of the unfairness that we face, and trying to gain resolution can be an exhausting and frustrating process. Prayer, on the other hand provides a direct line to the ultimate BMOC, without waiting in line or going through a succession of handlers. Kings 1, 8:45 says:

> Then hear Thou in heaven their prayer
> and their supplication.

This is a great reminder to realize that sometimes all you really need to do is open your heart to be immediately heard.

Pay Attention

I'M GOING TO SOUND CRANKY, but have you noticed how many people seem to be missing basic reading comprehension? Maybe it's because we're all inundated with endless requests coming in from all directions, and the nonstop demands of social media and more methods of communication. It seems as though people have all but stopped paying attention to what is said, and when and if they respond to a request, they frequently seem to have missed the point entirely. Nehemiah 1:11 says:

> *Let now Thine ear be attentive to*
> *the prayer of Thy servant.*

Wouldn't it be amazing if we could start every email or phone call or interaction with the same request? It would be great to be able remind people to be attentive to our needs. Maybe a good start would be vowing to be more attentive to others.

All Are Welcome in Prayer

I F YOU TAKE A GIANT STEP backward and banish any personal emotions from the equation, all prayer is the exact same, isn't it? Prayer is our deepest hopes and wishes put into words or set to music. And if you dig deep, you might find that the some of most famous holidays on the calendar have origins in, or similarities to, Pagan observance or harvest festivals. Yet there is so much strife and heartache throughout the world when it comes to matters of religion. Isn't it the most important thing that we're all people who believe? Isaiah 56:7 says:

> *My house shall be called a house of prayer*
> *for all peoples.*

I've felt shivers when I was at the Wailing Wall in Jerusalem, but I also felt incredibly moved in Downpatrick in Northern Ireland, the Vatican in Rome, and Sacré Coeur in Paris. I've walked the streets of Charleston, South Carolina, nicknamed the "Holy City" because of the proliferation of churches, and in the Holy Land of Israel, where three of the world's major faiths convene. To me the most important shared element was a shared belief in something higher than myself.

Be Delightful

I'VE ALWAYS LOVED the beauty ideals and fashions of other eras: the elaborate hairstyles of the Gibson girls, the bobs and Marceled hair and sleek fashion of the flappers, and my favorite of all, mid-century grooming and style. In fact, my first book was about beauty advertising from the 1940s through the '60s. The language in early advertising was quaint at best, and the enticements used were sometimes more than slightly insulting, though both were modern if not cutting-edge for the time. Proverbs 15:8 says:

> *The sacrifice of the wicked is an*
> *abomination to the Lord; but the*
> *prayer of the upright is His delight.*

Perhaps the concept of sacrifices is more than a bit odd for us, but I think that even if the wording feels arcane, we can understand the feeling behind prayer being a delight. Prayers don't only make us happy, but apparently, they make God happy as well.

Every Blade of Grass

IN THE BOOK OF HABAKKUK, Chapter 3 begins with a prayer of the prophet Habakkuk, in which he describes some of the beauty and power of God. And Verse 3 says:

The earth is full of His praise.

Don't you agree? It's hard not to notice all of the incredible beauty around us, from each and every individual blade of grass to the vividly hued fruits and flowers that spring up year after year. But more than that, on days when you feel as though you can't find the words to express your own joy at simply being alive, you have but to take a look around you to find true beauty and greatness in even the smallest of things.

Make an Action Plan

I N ANY BUSINESS or project management effort there are detailed action plans that must be created before they can be implemented. And perhaps a daily prayer book or outline can be considered a similar approach. Nehemiah 4:3 says:

> *But we made our prayer unto our God, and*
> *set a watch against them [our enemies]*
> *day and night, because of them.*

Like eating three meals a day, or going to the gym or Spring cleaning, having a plan and course of action can help you to reach your goals—even if it's the simple peace of daily quiet times and inner contemplation when you read through a chapter of the Psalms and close out the world for a few minutes a day.

Two-Faced Faith

THERE ARE MANY LAWS known to mankind. There are the Ten Commandments, which are commonly felt to be the tenets of most faiths. There are the laws of each nation and their particular rulers and complex legal systems. The common theme with each is adhering to set rules and ways of life. Proverbs 28:9 says:

He that turneth away his ear from hearing the law, even his prayer is an abomination.

Those who have changed their ways and seek forgiveness are always welcome, but the prayers of intentional scofflaws aren't welcome or solicited. Of course, we all make mistakes in our day-to-day lives; we're only human. But those who steal on a grand scale and then try to brush it off by tithing for charity aren't considered among the faithful, but rather distasteful on every level.

Active Prayer

I LOVE THE ART of crafts and am always trying out new techniques, stitches, and artistic pursuits. Some I stick with, some are just passing creative fancies. A couple of years back I tried to make retro-inspired lampshades. Needless to say, that wasn't my most successful endeavor. But as I made the actual paper from scraps of fabric that I ground down and blended, I felt as though I was weaving together bits of my own personal history into something newer and lovelier. Job 22:27 says:

> *Thou shalt make thy prayer unto Him,*
> *and He will hear thee.*

Whether you compose your own prayers out of your heartfelt wishes or needs, or whisper your own words to your God, you're composing your own prayers. And whether they include words of joy or oceans of tears, they will be heard.

Choose Wisely

I F YOU EVER READ accounts of ancient kingdoms or even historical fiction, you're sure to have read tales of intrigue and backstabbing and false attempts to create alliances with one's enemies. Jeremiah 11:14 says:

> *Therefore pray not thou for this people,*
> *neither lift up cry nor prayer for them;*
> *for I will not hear them in the time that*
> *they cry unto me for their trouble.*

The people in question are those who have stopped following the rightful path. From ancient prayer we can learn the wisdom or folly of creating relationships with those who have fallen out of favor or have willingly chosen the wrong path in life. It's sort of like the laws against aiding and abetting a criminal: if you help out a wrongdoer or pray on their behalf, you might just be putting your own best interests at risk.

Dressing Up

THERE ARE SO MANY LESSONS to be learned directly or indirectly from the various writings that make up the Old Testament. Queen Esther of ancient Persia, when going before her husband, King Ahasuerus, to beg for mercy on behalf of her people, fasted and prayed for three days before asking her husband for help. And the book of Esther 5:1 begins:

> *Esther put on her royal apparel, and stood in the inner court of the king's house.*

A few lines later it says, "When the king saw Esther the queen standing in the court, that she obtained favor in his sight." It seems such a simple thing to realize, but before asking for a big favor, or showing up to someone who can make major decisions with regard to your future, or simply entering a house of prayer, it's appropriate to dress up and show that you've made some effort.

Shared Faith

THE BOOK OF RUTH contains instances of incredible loyalty. Ruth's commitment to Naomi, the mother of her late husband, is notable for its poetic language. It's not a prayer proper, but rather a commitment and alliance that encompasses Naomi's faith as well. In Ruth 1:17, Ruth says to Naomi:

> *Entreat me not to leave thee, and to return*
> *from following after thee; for whither thou*
> *goest, I will go; and where thou lodgest, I*
> *will lodge; thy people shall be my people,*
> *and thy God my God.*

Ruth didn't make this declaration of shared faith based on comfort or ease, but rather because her belief compelled her forward on a shared path. Sometimes fervent belief can take the place of actual prayer. And that can mean learning as you go before setting out in a new direction.

In the Palm of His Hand

IT CAN BE HARD to declare that God loves us simply because we feel love for Him. But in Deuteronomy 33 there is a list of the blessings that Moses gave the children of Israel before his death. Verse 3 says:

> *He loveth the peoples, all His holy ones—*
> *they are in Thy hand; and they sit down at*
> *Thy feet, receiving of Thy words.*

It's incredibly comforting when the ancient prayers use language and imagery that even children can understand and relate to. What could feel better than being comforted and taken in hand—to sit cozily at the feet of someone you love and respect and to just take in their presence and learn from their wisdom? Sometimes the idea of a cozy relationship with God can be incredibly comforting in those cold or lonely times.

Prayer for the Departed

Part I

PRAYER DOESN'T HAVE TO BE a single act or method or interaction. And praying on behalf of someone else doesn't have to end because they've passed on. My neighbor Nadine was a lovely, gentle soul and a devoted wife and mother when she passed away after a brief but debilitating illness. I marvel at what an incredible job her husband, Juda, does at raising their two young children as a single father. And though she's been gone for a few years now, even veritable strangers remember Nadine fondly. A friend recently mentioned going to the cemetery to pray by her uncle's grave. And as she passed Nadine's grave, she stopped to pray there as well. The two have never met, yet Nadine's reputation in life carried through after her passing.

* * *

Part II

Jeremiah 31:14 says:

> *Thus saith the Lord: A voice is heard in*
> *Ramah, lamentation, and bitter weeping,*
> *Rachel weeping for her children;*
> *she refuseth to be comforted for her*
> *children, because they are no more.*

Rachel, the matriarch, died in childbirth while traveling, and she never lived to see her sons Joseph and Benjamin grow to be men. Rachel's husband, Jacob, heartbroken by the loss of his beloved wife, buried her on the road to Ephrath to serve as a future comfort for future generations in exile. It's said that when the children of Israel (quite literally, the children of Jacob, as Israel was another name for Jacob) were in exile and prayed to all of the patriarchs, their prayers weren't accepted, but as they passed the Tomb of Rachel, her spirit implored to God on behalf of her children and children's children. Though the loss of a loved one can leave such an incredible void in one's life, it's comforting to imagine that they're still looking out for you.

Brag, but Not About Being Bad

HAVE YOU EVER READ those stories about really stupid criminals who post online about their illegal escapades? I sometimes think that they have so little pride or that their accomplishments are so small and rare, that they'll brag even about the truly awful things they've done. Psalm 52:3 makes a great point in asking:

Why boastest thou thyself of evil?

I've noticed that a majority of people have a hard time sharing their accomplishments with others—not the silly things, but the ones with meaning, the ones they've worked hard for and should be crowing about. It can be difficult to decide on the right approach because modesty is definitely a virtue, yet self-promotion has become second-nature in our society. It's important to find a way to gracefully share your accomplishments with your loved ones and social circles. Just not the really bad ones!

Unexpected Blessings

Although I tend to be a very enthusiastic and positive person, I'm not someone who can find good in *every* single situation—many, but not all. That said, I do try to find a glimmer of hope in even the saddest of circumstances. In observant Jewish tradition, in addition to both a civil and religious marriage ceremony, both a civil and religious divorce ceremony are required as well. A close relative was heartbroken after his *Get* (the Aramaic word for the Jewish divorce ceremony) and was bewildered when the officiant who'd performed the ceremony came over to shake his hand and congratulate him. The smiling officiant gently explained that not everyone got to experience the commandment of giving a Get or to recite the accompanying blessing; and that my relative was doing the right thing and thereby was worthy of praise and congratulations. It was a bittersweet reminder that doing the right thing under tough circumstances is in itself a noble act deserving of recognition.

Long Distance Faith

I NEVER USED TO DISCUSS my religious background at all with people who didn't know me very well or hadn't known me for a really long time. After all, I was used to being viewed with suspicion if not outright disdain for retaining beliefs and practices passed down through my family for generations. People most often ask how on earth I can belief in a God that is at such a great distance and, in fact, in a realm I can't even fathom. Jeremiah 31:2 says:

From afar the Lord appeared unto me. Yea,
I have loved thee with an everlasting love;
therefore with affection have I drawn thee.

It reminds me of some long-distance relationships I've been in over the years. Before Skype and instant messaging, we still found ways to remain connected from afar. Some people don't have to attend church or synagogue services to feel connected; their belief and deep and abiding love are enough.

Bumps in the Road

I DON'T KNOW ABOUT YOU, but I hate fighting with people I love. I know realistically that when people are close to each other they can't always see eye to eye, but like many women, I kind of go along with things until they hit some sort of a boiling point. I'm always terrified, when I fight with my guy, that it's the end of us, despite the fact that he regularly and consistently reassures me otherwise. Isaiah 54 is a song sung to God and compares the relationship between God and his people to that of a husband and a wife. In 54:7–8 it says:

> *For a small moment have I forsaken thee;*
> *but with great compassion will I gather*
> *thee. In a little wrath I hid my face from*
> *thee for a moment; but with everlasting*
> *kindness will I have compassion on thee,*
> *saith the Lord thy redeemer.*

Like most relationships, your relationship with God can ebb and flow based on situations and circumstances. But that doesn't mean it's over; you're both in it for the long haul.

Everything Is Great— in Moderation

IF YOU READ SOMETHING out of context, you might have an entirely different interpretation of what the author is trying to say. For instance there's a portion in Ecclesiastes discussing the worst possible qualities to possess, including a detailed list of the action of fools. And in 10:19 it says:

> *A feast is made for laughter, and*
> *wine maketh glad the life; and*
> *money answereth all things.*

Well, it is more fun to enjoy a fun meal than an awkward one, and we all know that the occasional glass of wine shared with friends can be amazing, and who wouldn't be happier with a little more money? Someone once told me that problems that can be solved with money aren't actually problems at all. There's a lot of truth to that.

All Is Possible

Some people seem so anxious to see what the future brings, they forget about living in the present. Others become obsessed with things like their daily horoscope or palm readers or tarot or the many things that seem to provide an immediate if incredibly nebulous prediction fix. In Ecclesiastes 9:1, it's written:

> The righteous, and the wise, and
> their works, are in the hand of God;
> whether it be love or hatred, man
> knoweth it not; all is before them.

I don't know about you, but I like not knowing what the future holds. It's not that I love surprises—quite the opposite. (I actually ruined my own sweet 16 surprise party by showing up early to help set up.) But knowing what comes next spoils the enjoyment of the present. What if you knew that next Thursday at 6:45 p.m. would be the worst moment of your entire life? Would you be able to get through the week ahead? And what if you knew that night would be the best you'd ever have and it was all downhill from there? I prefer to discover all of life's ups and downs and in-betweens on my own.

The Five Scrolls

T HOUGH THEY ARE NOT comprised of prayers proper, the five Megillot, or scrolls, are part of the Old Testament writings (*ketuvot*) and read aloud during the prayer services of major holidays. The five scrolls are the Song of Songs, the Book of Ruth, the Book of Esther, the Book of Lamentations, and Ecclesiastes. It's fascinating to note that, in addition to including great stories and compelling life lessons, the scrolls also coincide with the times of the year, as well as the seasons of life. For me, it's also pretty amazing that two of the five include the stories of great women, Ruth and Esther. The ancient texts were full of stories of great heroines, such as the lesser known prophetess Huldah and the better known Miriam and Deborah, as well as the incredibly brave Queen Esther, loyal Ruth, and all of the other prophetesses and matriarchs who paved the way for strong women who followed.

Life Equals Hope

THE BOOK OF ECCLESIASTES, called *Kohelet* in Hebrew, is one of five scrolls (*megillot*), each of which is read on a different holiday. Ecclesiastes is read during the autumn harvest festival of Tabernacles, which feels appropriate because it's full of musing and wisdom—things many of us start to get into as the nights get longer and the year creeps toward and end. Chapter 9:4 says:

> *For to him that is joined to all*
> *the living there is hope; for a*
> *living dog is better than a dead lion.*

It's an interesting analogy, discussing being part of something larger than oneself and comparing a dog to a lion—one full of life and one defeated by it. It's easy to feel down as the leaves start to fall, but more important to realize that life goes on and, before you know it, spring will be on its way.

Don't Be Stingy with Praise

I'M A FIRM BELIEVER in giving people compliments. I'll rave about how fabulous my friends look and proudly share the great work of my talented friends. Hey, I've startled strangers on the street by telling them just how cute they look. I think that's why I can be so surprised when people aren't quick to offer a word of encouragement or praise. *Pesukai Dezimara*, Aramaic for "Chapters of Song" or "Hymnal Verses," are daily prayers comprising selections from the Psalms and other writings. One verse originates from Chronicles Book 1 16:9, and says:

> *Sing unto Him, sing praises unto Him;*
> *speak ye of all His marvellous works.*

In other circumstances the language might seem a bit repetitive, but in this instance it seems to encourage someone praying to be as over the top and generous with praise as possible. And maybe some of it will spill over into the person's daily interactions as well.

Find Happiness Within

ONE OF THE GREATEST PRESSURES in life is the constant pressure to find happiness. And that happiness seems to have the identical description for all people—it's bigger and it's shinier and more ostentatious than the happiness of your friends or neighbors. And that burden of trying always to be "on" and always be the accepted version of happy or happily-ever-after can actually rob you of the joy you've found in your own life. There's a line in the morning prayer service during the section dedicated to praise that translates to:

The heart of those who seek God
will be gladdened.

It probably isn't as simple as that—nothing ever is. But perhaps it's another empowering reminder to take solace in your faith. It just might bring you a level of happiness you never previously encountered.

Don't Brag about Being Better

HAVE YOU EVER READ something so beautiful in its simplicity that it almost felt like it actually was poetry or part of a prayer? I was reading through the Book of Zephaniah and came upon this line in Chapter 2:3:

> *Seek ye the Lord, all ye humble of the earth*
> *that have executed His ordinance;*
> *seek righteousness, seek humility.*

It's that last part that really got to me—to seek out a righteous path, to seek out a path of humility. It's not a concept of self-flagellation or putting yourself down in an insincere manner, but just emptying yourself of preconceived notions of what faith is. And while you're at it, don't brag either that you're a better person than everyone else. Knowing your own beliefs can be incredibly empowering, and you don't need everyone else's approval or admiration to be yourself.

Enduring Love

THERE ARE A LOT of people who believe that the love stories told in fiction reflect reality, and that the romantic comedies and happily-ever-after are what's real, as opposed to the incredibly hard work it is to maintain a loving ongoing relationship. There's a prayer in the daily service called *Yehi Kavod*, named for the first two words of the prayer, which translate to "May the Glory." The first line includes the sentence:

> *Blessed be the name of God, from this time and forever. From the rising of the sun until its setting, God's name is praised.*

If applied to a day-to-day relationship, this feels like a subtle reminder to remember the person you love and the reasons that you love them, throughout the day—not just when they cook your favorite foods or bring you flowers, but also when their snoring keeps you up all night or they forget your birthday.

Celebrating Imperfection

THERE'S A DAILY PRAYER called *Ashrei*, which means "happy" or "fortunate," that is mostly derived from various Psalms. It's said to have great spiritual significance when repeated three times daily. There's a small snippet of prayer that resonated with me:

His mercies are on all His works

The more obvious interpretation would be that God feels equally about all of his creations, perhaps tenderly and affectionately and akin to when a parent says that they have no favorites. But it also feels to me as though it means that God is perhaps not quite as judgmental as people are. His mercy isn't limited to the pretty or thin or rich or talented; we're all equal in his eyes. Along those lines, I've always loved imperfect art work: a hand-thrown pot with a fingerprint in it, or a handwoven rug with some mismatched threads. It's said that the rug makers in the Middle East used to weave errors into their most elaborate creations intentionally because they believed that only God is perfect.

Grape Expectations

ONE OF MY FAVORITE wine- and vine-related quotes is from the Talmud, and this prayer is frequently referenced in discussions of marriage or the search for a perfect match: *Invei Hagefen Be'invei Hagefen davar Na'ah Umitkabeil*, which translates better as a concept. The literal translation is that combining the grapes of one vine with the grapes of another vine is something pleasant and acceptable. It's an understated way of expressing the joy at two families joining together.

To take it a step further, my wine-wise friends tell me that the best vintages are those made by combining grapes from complementary vines, which then produce particularly flavorful wine. One more thought: grapes are among the few fruits that have the same blessings made over them as all fruits (*Borei pri ha'etz*) but when made into wine, there's another blessing entirely (*Borei pri ha'gafen*). It's a sweet metaphor to two people coming together and their union or even future offspring becoming even better than the sum of their parts.

Love and Regard

For some people, regular prayer isn't an option. Perhaps they're burnt out or need a new way of connecting or reconnecting with themselves or their faith. Some choose to read through some of the ancient texts for daily inspiration and believe Proverbs are a form of prayer. Proverbs 22:1 says:

*A good name is rather to be chosen
than great riches, and loving favor
rather than silver and gold.*

As anyone who grew up in a fairly strict environment can attest, protecting your reputation was something of a full-time job when growing up. Being polite to one's elders, dressing modestly, and doing the myriad things that most teens avoid was almost second-nature. And as we got older, reputation meant a coveted personal brand or self-defined rulebook that allows us to stand out from a crowd. This proverb reminds us that our investments in our own reputation and the high regard of our chosen peers are priceless.

Chased by Blessings

I DON'T KNOW ABOUT YOU, but there are some days when I feel like I'm paddling wildly in a sea of despair. Okay, perhaps I'm being slightly melodramatic, but there are days when it feels like I can't outrun my problems. This is probably part of the reason that I love this quote from Deuteronomy 28:2 so much:

And all these blessings shall come upon thee,
and overtake thee, if thou shalt hearken
unto the voice of the Lord thy God.

We generally know blessings as being things we think or say before eating, or things we count when we're feeling particularly fortunate. But I've never quite thought that if you do the right thing, the blessings might actually chase you down until they find you. I'll confess, the image of being chased down by overdue blessings puts a huge grin on my face!

Who's Your Guardian Angel?

P SALM 91 IS ONE of 11 Psalms attributed to Moses. Moses had such an eventful life, from a modest birth, to being adopted by the daughter of Pharaoh, to becoming a great leader and taking his people out of slavery in Egypt, to giving them the Ten Commandments. And while Moses had a direct line to communicate with God and the angels, he had a strong support network in the form of his brother Aaron, sister Miriam, and wife Zipporah. Verse 11 says:

> *For He will give His angels charge over thee,*
> *to keep thee in all thy ways.*

Most of us don't have quite that clear or direct a connection to our own God; so instead we rely on those who are closest to us to offer counsel and support—and they don't need wings or haloes to be the truly saving graces in our lives.

Personalized Blessings

PERSONALIZED GIFTS ARE incredibly popular for a reason. Whether someone has your initials embroidered on a T-shirt or inscribed on a piece of jewelry, or they choose your favorite color or scent, knowing they've taken your every preference into account makes a gift that much more precious. I was thinking about that while reading the following line in Genesis 49:28:

> All these are the twelve tribes of Israel, and
> this is it that their father spoke unto them
> and blessed them; every one according to
> his blessing he blessed them.

When Jacob blessed his 12 sons, he didn't offer each the same version of words previously shared with one of his other children; he tailored each one to the skills, preferences, and lifestyle of each and every one. And he didn't denigrate any of their unique abilities, but rather highlighted them as a precious quality. It's a great lesson always to see even those closest to you as unique human beings.

Az Yashir: Song of the Sea

*A*z Yashir translates to "Then [they] Sang." It is a rich and lyrical poem and a mainstay of daily prayer and liturgy services that first appears in the book of Exodus. It's also one of only two portions of the Old Testament that is typeset differently from the rest of prayer; it is set in two blocks of words with a significant margin in the center. Visually, it's meant to invoke the splitting of the sea, with room in the center for people to walk through. The second line begins with the simple words *Zeh Eli*, which translates to:

This is my God.

More than the incredible miracles and visual delights, these words seem elevated—a simple declaration of ownership, trust, and faith.

Who Is Like You?

I N THE MIDDLE of the morning prayers, there's an
excerpt that originally appears in Exodus 15:11:

Who is like you amongst the
heavenly powers? Who is like you,
glorious in holiness, awesome
in praises, doing wonders?

I really enjoy the excess praise in some of these
prayers. Think of the first time that you were in
love. Remember gushing to anyone who would listen about how wonderful the object of your affection was? That's what prayer feels like sometimes.
Being able to pour your heart out, every single
mushy emotion without fear of rejection or being
told you're becoming too needy or nudgy. We're for
the most part born creatures who thrive on regular
and ongoing affection. Society can teach us that it's
bad to ask for the love that you might not be receiving, or make us believe that we have to hide our
effusive and genuine selves. So go ahead, pour your
heart out in your next prayer. I promise that you
won't be rejected!

Everyday Exclamations

ARE THERE EVER WORDS or phrases that come to your mind so instinctively that you're sometimes not even aware of when you've actually said them? For me, those words include the phrase *Mah Rabu Ma'Asecha Hashem* or "How plentiful are Your creations, oh God." Though it's not commonly recited or part of the actual exhortation, the rest of the line is:

> *All of them You have made with wisdom—*
> *the earth is full of your creations.*

Though it's not officially a prayer, this passage springs to my lips several times daily, when I see the incredible gifts of nature: a perfect sunset, a baby bird, an extraordinary flower in bloom. These daily miracles that make me feel that the world might be a little less random and a little more filled with daily treasures.

A Smart Heart

THERE'S A PRAYER called *Ahavat Olam*, or "Eternal Love," which is a daily prayer (some say it in the morning, some consider it an evening prayer) that has portions that seem more poignant than most. One of the lines contains a few intertwined words with considerable impact. The person praying asks:

Instill deep understanding in our hearts.

Some people trust their gut instinct, relying on intuition to lead them in the right direction. Some people follow their head, allowing only clear logic to determine their course of action. Still others trust their heart, and for better or worse are guided by emotion. It would be a true gift to have a heart that understands the potential consequences of all actions and still retains its ability to love purely and completely.

Have Compassion

ONE OF THE THINGS that I love about the philosophy behind yoga is the notion of being in the moment: Refusing to allow daily worries and distractions to get in the way of your practice. Banishing the 10,000 random thoughts that are simultaneously clamoring for your attention, and instead committing to being fully present. But realistically in life, one's mind tends to wander. And some days you might be worried about paying the mortgage or about an ill relative, and before you know it, prayer time is over and you wonder if you should even have bothered. There's a prayer that's actually dedicated to the acceptance of prayer, and some of the words include:

Have compassion upon us and accept
our prayers in mercy and favor.

When you ask God to be compassionate to you, consider being a bit more compassionate to yourself. And try again tomorrow.

Anniversaries

A VARIATION OF THE PRAYER *Al HaNissim*, or "For the Miracles," is said during two holidays on the Jewish calendar: Purim and Chanukah. I've always been intrigued by the line *Bayamim Hahem Bazman Hazeh*, which translates to…

In those days, at this time

The phrasing always felt a bit enigmatic to me. The traditional interpretation might be recognizing the importance of commemorating significant anniversaries and momentous occasions in your personal or communal life. But it goes deeper. I think it's important to think about the obvious or unexpected miracles in your own life. Anniversaries aren't only for remembering the great things; sometimes your body unwittingly reminds you of a past illness or heartache, or of escaping a really bad situation. Sometimes miracles don't have to be obvious to be worth noting. Sometimes just remembering what once was or could have been and realizing just how much better you are in the here and now is reason enough to offer thanks.

Use Your Skills

THE STORIES OF ANCIENT REDEMPTION are frequently packed with great miracles and amazing tales of rescue. And while there are great lessons to be learned from these glorious tales, the truth is that we can't always wait for miracles; we have to be proactive in making our own lives better. When recounting the story of Purim—the joyous holiday created to celebrate Mordecai and Queen Esther's victory over the conniving Haman—there's very interesting language used. In the prayer discussing the miracles, the words *Hafarta et Atzato*, or:

> *You thwarted his ideas/counsel.*

This refers to Haman's evil plans to destroy Esther's people. It's one of the more unusual victories, because it relies on the planning and ideas of man and not the miracles from above. There's a great lesson here: sometimes the greatest miracles aren't the ones that most resemble magic, but the magic that your own logic and thought process can provide.

Be Your Own Best Interpreter

DREAMS PLAYED AN IMPORTANT PART in the stories of some of the patriarchs, from Jacob dreaming about ladders, to Joseph's thin cows and fat cows, and the bowing down sheaves of wheat. And I've always been struck by the notion that one of the takeaways of Joseph's rise to power in ancient Egypt was his ability to interpret dreams well—to offer clear analysis of what these dreams actually mean. I think of this in my own work sometimes in trying to analyze trends, not simply to speak what comes to mind, but to understand the deep meaning. There's a daily prayer that begins with the words *Vichol HaChayim Yoducha Selah*, or:

> *May all living beings praise You.*

This is a wonderful thought about everything on earth, from a blade of grass to a human being, finding a way to praise its maker. But the Hebrew word *Chayim* doesn't just mean "living," it also means "life." And so when I reread this prayer and made notes for myself, I initially thought it meant "For all of your life," which theoretically could be an equally accurate interpretation—not to be fickle in your faith, but to keep strong to your belief for your entire life, despite the vagaries and temptations of external influences.

Stars in Your Eyes

B Y THE TIME YOU'VE READ through the entire Book of Psalms, you've likely noticed many recurring themes and frequently repeated language. Despite the fact that the Psalms were composed by some of the greatest figures in history, the human mind is finite and can only come up with so many rapturous descriptors. In Psalm 148:3 the psalmist says:

> *Praise ye Him, sun and moon;*
> *praise Him, all ye stars of light.*

It's a phenomenal image, all of the brightest elements in our universe paying homage to God. And it makes me think of all of the incredible sunsets and starry nights—all technically the same, but all so incredibly different. Sometimes certain themes are repeated because they best describe the nearly indescribable.

Use Your Five Senses

THERE'S A CEREMONY made at the end of every Sabbath, and after many Jewish holidays, called *Havdalah* or "Separation." Depending on how you look at it, the ceremony marks either the end of the Sabbath or the beginning of the week ahead. And there are many symbolic elements to the ritual, including a blessing made over wine and the smelling of sweet spices, usually cloves. It's said that the ceremony requires people to engage all five of their senses, from listening to the blessings, to tasting of the wine, to the smelling of the spices, to viewing the flickering candles and feeling their warmth. It's a wonderful reminder not simply to sleepwalk your way through your work week, no matter how difficult or boring it might feel. Life is for living, so finding a single way to engage your senses during a typical day can transform even the most ordinary of moments. Don't just stop and smell the roses; inhale deeply and take the scent with you through your day.

Family Blessings

THERE'S A SHORT Yiddish phrase my mother says without fail every Saturday night, either after hearing the *Havdalah*, or Separation ceremony, or just to usher in the week ahead—*Zul Zayn Voyl*, or:

It should be good.

These four short words always feel to me like the most meaningful blessing or benediction possible. Though it isn't any kind of official prayer or any well-recognized saying, in our family no week can fully end or begin without us saying or hearing these words. I sometimes wonder where traditions or customs become legend, and how they evolve over generations. And some traditions can feel as important as elements of faith that have been passed throughout the centuries. Words without meaning are just words, and sometimes the meaning behind a few simple words can mean more than the prayers of an entire congregation.

Years of Blessings

THERE'S A PRAYER in the morning services that seems to be pretty farreaching, yet it actually deals with the urgencies of everyday life. *Birkat Hashanim*, or the "Blessings of the Years," begins by asking for help with crops, which in ancient parlance might have meant the difference between life and death. Today, most people have moved past dependence on immediate agricultural successes or failures for their day-to-day existence, so it's the larger themes that matter most. The prayer ends with the words:

> *Blessed are You oh, Lord*
> *who blesses our years.*

I sometimes feel like there are words that in their simplicity sum up our greatest desires. We might ask for health and love and good fortune, but we mean that we hope our years, our lives, remain blessed.

A Faithful Heart

I**N ADDITION TO ORIGINAL** compositions, the daily prayer service is sprinkled with excerpts from different sources. In the daily morning prayers, there's one called "And David Blessed," which includes sections from the book of Nehemiah. A small portion from Chapter 9:8 references Abraham and includes the words:

> *And you found his heart true [faithful]*
> *before you.*

Even the most noble souls of more recent generations can't hope to compare themselves to the devotion and commitment of Abraham and the forefathers. But we can be strongly influenced by their finest attributes. Self-help books would have you believe that you need to change yourself from the top down to become a better person. But what if you concentrated on one trait only? Building a truer heart helps you become more impervious to external pressures or falsely popular trends. Trust your heart to know what's truly important.

Look Down, but Don't Be Aloof

There are several prayers in the daily services that include or begin with the words *Habeit Mayshamayim*, which means:

Look down from the heavens.

Depending on the prayer that follows, the words are either a cry to God for help or attention—please look down at us and don't forget about us—or a plea not to hold yourself up and away from us. On some level, it also feels like beseeching God not to be aloof, which also is a great lesson for the rest of us. Success shouldn't make you forget the people you once rubbed shoulders with or used to consider friends. And if you are the kind of person who does really well in life and remembers your community, don't act like you're better than others. Because, as the old saying goes: Remember the people you meet on the way up; they'll be the same people that you meet on the way down.

The Brotherhood of Suffering

THE WORDING OF SOME PRAYERS make them feel appropriate on a daily basis and also for special occasions. *Acheinu*, or "Brotherhood," can be said on a daily basis and also sung on the Sabbath. But it isn't a warm and fuzzy "Kumbaya"-type ditty; it's more a prayer of remembrance and unity. And the words implore God to remember those:

> *...who are in distress and captivity,*
> *who wander over sea and over land—*
> *may God have mercy on them, and*
> *bring them from distress to comfort.*

No matter how well your own life might be going, there might be some close to you who are still suffering. It's important to keep those less fortunate than you in mind and prayer.

Song of the Day

FOR THE UNINITIATED or those finding their way back to prayer, I like to offer the option of reciting the daily prayers on an a la carte basis. Start with one or two prayers that most resonate with you and build to a complete daily routine. Although there are daily prayers, or ones coinciding with calendar dates and special occasions, there are also those that can serve as stand-alones or prayers that can be combined with others to form your own version of a daily service. The *Shir Shel Yom*, or "Song of the Day," are short excerpts from the Book of Psalms that are said at the closing portion of the daily prayer services. The chosen sections correspond to the days of creation. If the day of rest is the high point of the week, then each day's songs act as a countdown to the Sabbath as well.

Compassion Even in Victory

MANY OF THE ANCIENT PRAYERS, most especially those derived from biblical texts include tales of great victories over enemies. And while defeating one's greatest adversaries is definitely cause for celebration, it should always be tempered with humanity. I always think about this quote from Proverbs 24:17: *Binpol Oyvecha Al Tismach*, or:

> *Do not rejoice at the fall of your enemy.*

While the immediate reaction to overcoming adversity is relief, if not giddiness, it's also important to realize that your enemies and their families might be suffering greatly. And any amount of suffering in the world is a bad thing, much less if you're the one causing the pain. Joy that is a result of someone else's pain leaves a twinge—as well it should.

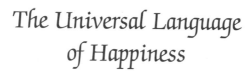

The Universal Language
of Happiness

SINCE ANCIENT TIMES there have been seven blessings traditionally said during Jewish wedding ceremonies that are still said to this day. These prayers have also been adapted to modern wedding ceremonies in numerous nationalities. My favorite of the seven blessings includes the words *Sameach TeSamach Re'im Ahuvim*, which includes a double wish for happiness for the beloved couple:

> *Be happy and rejoice.*

It's amazing how the language of love and happiness can be almost universal. These words bring to mind the words "Dearly Beloved," which begin many wedding ceremonies, as well as the Chinese notion of "Double Happiness" as a blessing. For many people the absolute obsession of having a perfect wedding overshadows the importance of having a happy marriage. Here's hoping that, for most people, the happiness of the day lasts throughout their shared lives.

The Prayers of Others

WHEN I WAS DEEP in the midst of my battle with cancer and undergoing four types of chemo, I cried myself to sleep every single night. I felt bewildered and trapped within my own body. My soul was depleted, and as I searched my heart and thought through my life and relationship with God, I was angry. I felt furious and lost and betrayed and wondered why I had believed in a God who could not only desert me, but also inflict such a horrible disease on me—one with a cure that sometimes felt even worse than the cancer itself. It says in the Talmud (Baba Kamma 92a) that:

> *He who asks mercy for another*
> *while he himself is in the same need,*
> *will be answered first.*

As I felt so desolate and alone, I wondered if my years of praying for everyone else and putting my own hopes last, had left me vulnerable. And yet as I finally healed, I realized so clearly that it wasn't my faith that had gotten me through; I had none left at that point. It was the faith of others that pushed me through when I felt as though I couldn't take another step forward. Even when you feel as though you're just going through the motions and questioning your own faith and beliefs, you have no idea of whose faith you might be strengthening with your own. And some days, when you feel like your prayers haven't been heard or answered, realize that sometimes it's the people around you that most need your faith.

Hallel: Praise

THERE ARE MANY ancient prayers that either begin with words that are variations of *Hallel*, or "praise," are relegated to the realm of a group of praise-related prayers, or simply offer praise and thanks to God. One in particular, in the Praise services said on holidays, is an excerpt from Psalm 113 and includes the words:

[He who] raises the desperate and destitute
from the dust.

It's powerful stuff and steeped in a greater message and lesson. When you feel beaten down by life, it's hard to find anything to be grateful for. And when the dust settles and you're feeling more like yourself, you can find endless amazing things in what most people might find ordinary. So on those days when it just feels too hard to feel hopeful, give yourself permission to slack off, and when you're back to yourself, let loose and fill your heart and world with gratitude.

Thoughts on Revenge

IF YOU LEAF THROUGH the different parts of the Old Testament, you'll notice God described in many different ways: A loving God, a generous God, a jealous God, a merciful God, a vengeful God. And on some level, that feels great. When people take advantage of you, or worse, wage a literal war against everything that you stand for, you can rely on your God to take vengeance for you. But who are we kidding? Revenge and vengeance are not endeavors to be taken lightly, because the anger that drives us and the machinations involved can eat away a person from the inside out. In the daily prayer for Wednesday, there's an excerpt from Psalms 94:1:

> Oh Lord, to whom vengeance belongs;
> Oh God, to whom vengeance belongs-
> show thyself.

Maybe it's better to leave the vengeance to the fates and live your life the right way.

Don't Be Afraid

THERE'S A PRAYER CALLED *Al Tira*, or "Don't be afraid," that's part of the daily services, a prayer said to stave off night terrors and a mainstay during times of great fear. Unfortunately, over the past few years we've become far too accustomed to hearing about acts of terror that claim human life on a grand scale. It's nice to have a prayer or words that instantly reassure you, or remind you that despite awful events, life goes on and so should you. The first line of the prayer is:

> *We will have no fear of*
> *the suddenness of terror.*

Maybe the lesson here is to focus on the suddenness of the terror. Fear compounds fear. So trying to remain calm and move forward with life helps us to reconnect with the comfort of a daily routine.

Prayers for Livelihood

THERE'S A PRAYER CALLED *Parshat Haman*, or the "Prayer on the Manna," that some people say every day to ensure financial prosperity. There's also a tradition of saying it on one special day of the year; the formula for explaining that particular date is a bit complicated, but it's usually sometime in January or early in the year. There's another one called "Prayer for Livelihood," which can be said every day but the Sabbath and holidays. It includes excerpts from Nehemiah, Exodus, and Deuteronomy, and there's some wonderful phrasing, including the words:

> *He brought food from the heavens*
> *and water from the rock.*

This alludes to the manna and the water Moses produced by hitting a rock, and some gentle requests as well:

> *Nourish us, sustain us, support us,*
> *and supply all of our needs.*

Most of all, we ask that it be:

> *Abundant, with fullness and generosity and*
> *without great toil or exertions.*

Good News/Bad News

A s I was looking through the prayers said on special occasions, I noticed a great deal of similarity between a blessing said upon hearing unusually good news, and one said when hearing very sad news. The first includes the words *Ha'Tov U'Maitiv*, meaning:

> Who is good and does good.

This is said when you hear about great news that benefits either yourself or another. The second is said when you hear about a death: *Baruch Dayan Ha'Emet*:

> Blessed is the true judge.

I used to wonder about the seemingly mild-mannered words in the latter. After all, the Old Testament is full of stories of rending one's clothing, and wearing sackcloth and ash. Shouldn't the blessing match the emotion? Having lived through many highs and incredible lows, I realize that both of these blessings reflect an acceptance. Not everything is in our control, and learning to accept the roller coaster of life is a blessing in and of itself.

Welcome to the World

I N THE COURSE of the average day, there are words that spring to people's lips so frequently that they might not realize that they might also be used as blessings or the beginnings of blessings. When guests arrive, or even when a welcome friend comes to your house, it's customary to say *Baruch Habah*, or:

> *Blessed is he who arrives.*

There are several variations of the same blessings based on sex, since Hebrew is a gender-specific language. It also made me go "Awww" to read that this is a common greeting that the entire congregation makes in unison to a baby boy when he is brought into the room on the morning of his circumcision. While there's controversy surrounding the notion of circumcisions, there can be no dispute around the fact that it's a wonderful notion to afford an eight-day-old baby the same respect given an esteemed guest.

The Ten Percent Solution

THE BOOK OF RUTH includes instances of Terumah or the concept of tithing, where it was customary to leave a percentage of one's crop for the poor. Ruth went to the fields of Boaz, who was known to be generous with the poor. There's actually a process and blessing involved that includes the words:

To separate gifts and tithes

Tithing is traditionally giving 10 percent of one's earnings to charity; of course, giving more or generously is a greater act of kindness. But giving never goes out of style and crosses faiths and generations. I learned from my friend Connie that in her Mormon Church, members fast one day each month and then donate the money they would have spent on food to the needy—yet another way of translating ancient prayers and faith to modern life.

The Work of Our Hands

F OR A VERY SMALL CHILD, there were few feelings comparable to the pride of having your mother hang your latest masterpiece on the refrigerator door. But as you get older it becomes harder to find ways to share your pride in accomplishment in quite the same way. When you're an adult, projects are a team effort, or they're less hands-on, and unless you become an artist or craftsperson, your accomplishments aren't publicly displayed. There's a prayer called *Vayehi Noam* or "Let it be pleasant," which is said before bed or on Saturday nights and includes part of Psalm 90. The words feel somewhat complicated, but in reading many different translations it feels as though the person praying is asking God to ensure that whatever they do is successful:

> *Let the kindness of the Lord our God*
> *be with us. Make us successful in*
> *everything we do. Yes, make us*
> *successful in everything we do.*

We try hard to do the right thing and hope we're successful, and with a little help from above, we might just be.

Every Day a Blessing

I**T CAN BE EASY** to be a person of strong faith when everything is going your way. Peppering conversations with "Thank God" and "I feel blessed" is second-nature during the good times, but much less so when you're mired in daily struggles that wear you down. And having faith is not quite as effortless when every day feels harder than the one that came before. In the daily prayer *Elohai Neshamah*, or "My God, the Soul," there's a wonderful line:

> *All the time that my soul is within me,*
> *I give thanks.*

So many people put their lives on hold until the day when things get better. They'll celebrate when the mortgage is paid off or when legal dealings are completed. But isn't every single day that you're breathing a reason to celebrate? Try finding something tiny to celebrate today; it might make tonight a little easier to bear.

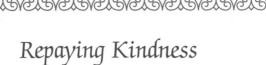

Repaying Kindness

I'M ONE OF THOSE PEOPLE who derives great pleasure and satisfaction from doing nice things for other people. It gives me genuine happiness to be able to do a random act of kindness without any kind of expectation of repayment. And yet, conversely, I hate feeling taken advantage of or not appreciated. How can I resolve my inner dichotomy? I'm not sure that I can. And I'm not sure that I should have to. Just as it feels really great to be able to do something nice for others, it feels awful not to have your best efforts acknowledged. In the praise portion of the daily prayers there's a section derived from Psalm 116 that goes:

> *How can I repay unto the Lord*
> *all His bountiful dealings toward me?*

Well, you can't. But in praying, you can at least show appreciation and recognition for what you do have.

I Am My Prayer

ONE OF THE SWEETER morning prayers, *Mah Tovu*, "How Goodly [are your tents]," concludes with a line beginning with the words *Va'ani Tefilati*, which translates to:

> *I am my prayer.*

I'm not sure that I can begin to express to you just how much I love that line. It brings to mind, for me at least, Rabbi Yisroel ben Eliezer, better known as the *Ba'al Shem Tov* ("Man of the Good Name"), a seventeenth-century mystical rabbi who believed that an appreciation of the beauty of nature was akin to great prayer. I believe it was he who said that one should look at the swaying trees and realize this is their method of prayer. I think of Walt Whitman's poem "I Hear America Singing," which speaks of the unique carols of carpenters and shoemakers and woodcutters: "Each singing what belongs to him or her and to none else." While ancient prayer can serve as inspiration, you don't always need complicated words or phrasing to express your soul.

Know When You're Done

ALTHOUGH I'M NOT a perfectionist in all things, I tend to get obsessive about getting most details right—sometimes a little too obsessive. It can be hard to end a project or stop decorating a cake and just let it go. On Friday night, before *the Sabbath meal there's a ceremony and prayer* known as *Kiddush*, said just before the blessing on the wine. One of the lines made me realize how important it is to recognize when things are done— or done well enough:

> *And on the seventh day God completed His work that He had done.*

It serves as inspiration to me to let my perfectionism go. If God created a world in six days and was satisfied enough with his work not to keep going, it's important for the rest of us to realize that sometimes you just have to let something go and hope and imagine that you've done as well as you could.

Strong Endings

THERE'S A CUSTOM to recite a certain short saying when you either finish reading every book of the Old Testament through weekly readings, or you complete the reading of all five books. The saying is *Chazak, Chazak, V'Nitchazak*, which means:

Be strong, be strong and be strengthened.

There are varied interpretations of when this custom began; some say it started in twelfth-century France, while others believe it became popular in Poland sometime during the sixteenth century. It's also said that the three-part strengthening was inspired by blessings in the book of Joshua. Whatever the origin, it's a complex prayer whose words and meanings are intertwined. Much in the way that learning the great books strengthens a person's knowledge and faith, the knowledge also strengthens community and family ties. And in an endearing way, we strengthen the good books and knowledge base as well with our support in keeping it all alive over the generations.

Acknowledgments

OH, I AM A LUCKY WOMAN. I have so many people who love me and support me and believe in me, even when I sometimes forget to believe in myself.

My love and thanks to:

My father, David, who jokingly refers to himself as my research assistant for a good reason, and my mother, Judith, who inspires me with a lifelong love affair with books. My parents generously shared with me their insatiable curiosity about the world, love of learning, and ongoing thirst for knowledge.

My sister, Kiki, who is a one-woman cheering team and endless font of inspiration. (You wish you had a sister like her!)

My brother, Jay, for taking his little sister to the library every Friday without fail.

My gratitude to my brilliant editor and champion, Andrea M. Rotondo, former Barnes & Noble buyer Michelle Faulkner, and the entire team at Sterling Publishing and Barnes & Noble.

My wonderful friends and treasured tribe composed of people who over the years have nurtured me—body, heart, mind, and soul: Sonia Brown, Iyna Bort

Caruso, Anthony Elia, Heidi Fischer, Beth Hughes, Anne Isenhower, Jen Joseph, Phil Katz, Peninah Merzel, Angela Musolino, Connie Myers, Ken Paulin, Maria Perez, Jennie Phipps, Erik Sherman, Lewis Silverman, Blossom Steinberg, and Neal Tully.

And Lewis, who frequently reminds me what happiness means.

And everyone who's ever sent up a good thought, lit a candle, burned some incense, or recited a prayer on my behalf.

And you. On the days that you doubt and still believe, on the days when you're not sure that your words are heard, your prayers have power. I believe in you.

Some Final Thoughts
on Ancient Prayers

I DEBATED MIGHTILY WITH MYSELF about whether or not to include entire prayers and translations. I also wasn't sure how much of each prayer to include. Because this book is meant to offer food for thought and comfort, along with inspiring thoughts or sparks of thought and introspection, I include excerpts, translations, or quotes when appropriate—sometimes in both Hebrew and English. (I will mention if a prayer is in a different language such as Yiddish or Aramaic.) Because ancient/biblical Hebrew differs significantly from modern Hebrew and is a tough language to master, I tried to translate in a way that felt right to me. And as I spoke with more people about their own thoughts on prayer, I realized just how lucky I am to understand the words I say, to connect to the meaning within the sounds.

Another issue I faced was the issue of an all-encompassing God. Many of the original prayers refer to the "God of Israel." I consulted with friends and clergy members of many varying faiths and came to the following conclusion: As faiths and religions progressed over the centuries, it became more commonly accepted to realize that the God of Israel is more of an all-encompassing deity for anyone embracing Judeo/Christian-inspired beliefs—or even for anyone seeking ancient wisdom to inspire them on a daily basis. And because this book touches more on the ancient and original prayers and thoughts behind them, rather than any specific religion, I felt it appropriate to leave that reference in when possible.

Another issue that I struggled with was whether or not to include God's name spelled out and in its various forms. There are those who believe that any variation of the name should not be spelled out, but rather appear with dashes in place of key letters: G-d, for instance. In traditional prayer books and other holy liturgy and tracts, the name and its variations are fully spelled out. I've chosen that route for this book as well, because it makes the prayers more authentic and empowering. But that gives readers a responsibility as well. Books with religious words and meanings are generally forbidden for use in the bathroom. And if pages become well-worn or tattered from use, there is a tradition called *Sheimos/Shaimos* (literally translated from a Yiddish variation of the Hebrew word for "names") or *Geneezah*, the Hebrew word for "treasure." The notion is that books or objects that are considered holy but can no longer be used should not be treated as common trash. Worn out Torah scrolls are afforded a very particular method of burial, for instance. So, I ask

that you treat this book kindly and with a level of respect you might deem worthy of your other books relating to faith or prayer.

I also want to mention a small detail: When transliterating Hebrew to English, there's the option of representing the guttural 'ch' sound (similar to those found in Germanic or Gaelic languages) in English in several ways, with a "Ch" or "H" (as in Chanukah/Hanukkah) or a "Ch" vs. a "Kh" as in *L'Chaim*. I opted for the "Ch" in most situations, because it felt more organic and natural, but it's just personal choice.

One last thing: Though this book deals with prayer, it is in no way meant to be a religious guide or substitute for any kind of prayer book or tract. My hope is that *Ancient Prayer* will offer some timeless and universal examples of inspiring words that have endured throughout the ages.

About the Author

RACHEL WEINGARTEN IS KNOWN for her uncanny ability to analyze and predict big trends, yet she remains firmly grounded in lessons learned from the past—both recent and ancient. As a child she learned to read, write, and recite all of her daily prayers in the original Hebrew and Aramaic. Rachel is both a writer and brand and marketing strategist. Her multifaceted professional background includes working in the diamond industry, as a celebrity makeup artist, founding early Internet start-ups, and creating and acting as the on-air talent for a show on CNN Money. Rachel is the author of *Career and Corporate Cool* and *Hello Gorgeous! Beauty Products in America, '40s–'60s*. She's a weekly style columnist for Parade.com and an opinion columnist for *am New York* and writes for or has been quoted by top outlets including ABC News, AP, CNN, *Crain's New York Business*, Esquire.com, *Fortune*, NPR, the *New York Times*, and the *Wall Street Journal*. Rachel is a popular public speaker and teaches or leads seminars on the graduate level at top universities, including FIT and NYU. Rachel is a Brooklyn native and harbors a particular fondness for local history.